The Haunted Journey

The Haunted Journey

by Robert Murphy

DOUBLEDAY & COMPANY, INC.
Garden City, New York, 1961

Acknowledgment is made to Holt, Rinehart and Winston, Inc., The Society of Authors and Jonathan Cape, Ltd., for permission to reprint lines from *Last Poems, XII,* by A. E. Housman. Copyright 1922 by Holt, Rinehart and Winston, Inc. Copyright 1950 by Barclay's Bank Ltd.

For Jeannie, Molly and Shane

After traversing nearly 700 miles in a fog so thick that we could scarcely see 50 yards at any time, a northeast wind cleared things for a few hours, and . . . we saw the high mountains of Kamchatka.

—Captain Beechey, of His Britannic Majesty's Navy, who in 1832 sailed the seas where we are going in this book.

And how am I to face the odds
Of man's bedevilment and God's?
I, a stranger and afraid
In a world I never made.

—Last Poems
A. E. Housman

Fortuna arbitriis tempus dispensat iniquis.

Ovid

In 1646 A party of *promyshleniki,* wild and rugged characters who wandered about the grim and empty wastes of subarctic Siberia in search of fur and mammoth tusks, set out from the palisaded fort of Nizhne-Kolymsk to sail about on the Arctic Ocean. Nizhne-Kolymsk was a government post near the mouth of the Kolyma River, the last large river to the east on the northern Siberian coast, and a very long way from anywhere; it was the point of furthest penetration in that country, but the *promyshleniki* wanted to go even farther; there were rumors in East Siberia that there were islands somewhere out in the Frozen Sea which were covered with mammoth ivory, and they wanted to find them. Wood was extremely scarce on that coast, so they found several driftwood logs, hollowed them out, made bulwarks of driftwood planks held together with willow twigs and reindeer sinew, stitched up some hides into a sail and set out. There was so much drift ice and so many bergs about that they couldn't move very far, and finally gave up their search. But after they came ashore they encountered a party of Chukchi, the natives of that country who were cousins of the Eskimoes, a tough and independent race who were always ready to fight and could hold their own against anybody; almost alone among the tribes of Siberia they had soundly beaten any group of Cossacks who had ever tried conclusions with them. Oddly enough, these Chukchi were inclined to trade rather than fight at the moment, so the *promyshleniki* got some walrus ivory from them.

Walrus ivory was in demand, and when the *promyshleniki* got back to Nizhne-Kolymsk, there was talk of organizing another

9

party. As there was profit in it, and as the government at Moscow was always curious about Siberia, the official in charge of the post asked for a government representative to go with them. He was given a Cossack named Semon Deshneff.

Deshneff, who would have been an ornament to any company of rugged adventurers, took charge of the new party. They built another boat much like the one the first party had built, and in this ramshackle contrivance they set out on an expedition that has since given the historians a good deal of trouble. There has been much argument about it, but it seems to be accepted now that they sailed around East Cape, the easternmost point in Asia, and reached the Anadyr River—the most northern of the rivers on the Bering Sea. It was a journey of 1200 miles or so, and couldn't possibly have been done if the Arctic Ocean hadn't been extraordinarily free of ice that year; at any rate, it demonstrated that there was no land connection between Asia and the North American continent.

Deshneff's accomplishment, entailing fearful hardships, is all the more remarkable because he had no money to back him and no equipment. He had started from a newly established and forlorn little outpost that was a thousand miles from anywhere in a cruel and unknown land peopled with hostile savages; he had no idea where he was going and apparently no worries as to whether he would ever get back again. He constantly faced storms and starvation; his boat was wrecked near the Anadyr, and after wandering about until they were almost dead, he and his party were found by a few natives, who carried them through the winter. In the spring he asked his rescuers for *yassak,* tribute for the Russian crown; when it was refused he ordered the natives slaughtered.

He ultimately made a report of his trip to the governor at Yakutsk, the capital of East Siberia; and although the Russians, as well as the rest of the civilized world, wanted to know whether Asia and America were joined, and what the North Pacific looked like, the report was pigeonholed until 1736—nearly a hundred years.

The Haunted Journey

chapter
one

Toward the end of the year 1724 Peter the Great, that
bear of a man nearly seven feet tall who had decided to westernize
Russia, took to his bed to die in St. Petersburg. The raw new city,
with its many canals, straight, wide, windy streets and great
wooden palaces designed by Italian architects, which he had
founded in 1703 among the swamps along the Neva and built
on pilings, was shrouded in its usual winter gloom. Five hours
of cold gray daylight was the most that could be counted on at
that time of year and usually more than it got, for the freezing
fogs from the Gulf of Finland usually blotted out what little sun
the surly overcast sky let through.

Despite the winter weather and the dying Czar, there was a
good deal of gaiety in the town, at least among the aristocrats
who were in favor, the rich merchants and the high government
officials. It was a boorish sort of gaiety, with a great deal of heavy
drinking and wild gambling going on, rather looked down upon
by the foreign colonies that had increased during Peter's reign,
for the foreigners viewed the Russians as savages all too lately
brought out of a sort of Asiatic barbarism by ukase rather than by
their own cultural development. There was practically no middle

class. The population was either noble or serf, and the nobles spent most of the time in the great hot baths, in resplendent visits or at parties. The single bridge across the Neva, built on boats, was taken up in winter, and anyone who wanted to cross the river crossed it on the ice. It was not a pretty city, for not much had been done to beautify it and wouldn't be for another twenty years, and there was a good deal of hidden discontent; for a great many people suspected the foreigners who had been thrust upon them and didn't hold at all with changing the old ways. There was nothing overt done about this discontent, however, although Peter was a cruel, determined and violent man, an autocrat who stopped at nothing; and on clear days anyone could see the thin golden spire of the Fortress of St. Peter and St. Paul across the river and remember that although it had originally been built as a fortress, it was now an infamous prison where Peter had ordered his own son put to death, and into which anyone who acted upon his discontents with the regime would disappear and never be heard of again.

That Peter had to be brutal to carry out his plans for Russia was probably unavoidable, for the people were lazy, ignorant and immoral; crime flourished, murder was a commonplace, and thousands of illegitimate babies were born yearly, most of which were quickly done away with until Peter forbade infanticide under pain of death and ordered homes established for these children throughout Russia. Drunkenness was everywhere, and not only among the poor; the nobles and the clergy drank even more because they could better afford to do it. During some of the religious holidays that fell in the winter, wagons collected the corpses, often gnawed by dogs during the night, of drunks who had fallen asleep in the snow, as they wandered about, and frozen to death.

Women were chattels and frequently beaten, and corruption was commonplace in government and elsewhere. There wasn't sufficient money to pay the lower civil servants enough to live on, and they were expected to take bribes and steal. The thievery didn't end with them, however. It ran through all ranks, and Menshikov, Peter's most trusted advisor and the richest man in Russia, stole more than anybody else. Corruption may have been common all over Europe at this time, but in Russia it was the way of life. Peter's ukases against it brought into being secret police called "fiscals," who were the most hated men in Russia; and they in their turn encouraged informers and anonymous letter writers. They had no connection with the Secret Office— the foundation for the Cheka, the OGPU and the MVD—which had been established earlier in Peter's reign and expanded after his westernization program got under way because of the almost universal hatred in which it was held.

The sinister agents of these two organizations were everywhere and brought down their quarry no matter whether he was a serf, a senator or a governor of Siberia. They and their works— the public hangings and impalings, the secret tortures, the unfortunates who had their tongues burnt out with hot irons or were knouted, beheaded or broken alive on the wheel—were as much a part of the scene as the great new buildings lining the clear blue waters of the Neva, the cold fogs, Peter sailing on the river in summer in his little boat or some old peasant woman muttering that the Czar was anti-Christ because he had ordered that people must wear European clothes.

In this atmosphere the parties went on, with a sort of barbaric splendor, and in the Winter Palace Peter was working fitfully upon his final project, which he considered very important for the future of Russia. He had long wanted to know the confines of his empire to the east and whether it joined with America, but he had never heard of Deshneff's journey around East Cape or of his report. He had always encouraged the Cossacks in their far-ranging wanderings over Siberia, but even with his terrible vitality and his wish to find a short cut of his own to China he hadn't been able to get around to doing more. In 1715, when he had visited Europe, the members of the French Academy and a number of other scientific men had approached him to settle the question of whether the continents of Asia and America were joined and to clear up the complete obscurity which then held regarding the geography of the North Pacific. They had even asked him for clearance to send an expedition of their own to Kamchatka and the unknown sea, but Peter had refused them, saying that he would send an expedition of his own.

The geographers of the day were in complete confusion about this region; to them it contained land masses seen through fogs or storms or supposedly seen by earlier seafarers. Two lands, called Gamaland and Companyland—the first after a Spanish sailor named Don Juan de Gama and the second after the Dutch East India Company—began to appear on the maps. Every cartographer put these lands where he thought they should be until Guillaume Delisle, the foremost geographer of the day, decided in 1720 that Kamchatka, which was still unexplored in the south, was close to Japan, and Gamaland and Companyland were not far from it. All of these various maps, abetted by the maps, globes and reputation of the great Delisle, had firmly impressed upon the prevailing thought of the time that these imaginary lands were not imaginary at all but real, and that perhaps one of them was America.

Peter had long wondered about the limits of his empire, but he had been too occupied to do much about finding out about it. From the beginning of his reign, which had started in 1689, when he was seventeen, through a *coup d'état* engineered by himself and his mother's family, the Naryshkins, he had been turning Russia upside-down and getting embroiled in wars with Turkey and Sweden, an uprising of the Guard Regiments, the backbone of the army, at home and another uprising among the Cossacks on the Don River. These wars and uprisings, with the intrigue, diplomacy and responsibilities of leadership which went with them, would have been enough to occupy most men, but Peter hadn't been in the least like most men.

He had reorganized the army along European lines before the wars began, and reorganized it again as they went along. He reorganized the judicial and administrative departments of the government as well, although his efforts in these branches were a sort of patchwork because there was never enough money and because the changes were so unpopular. He had spent some time working alongside shipwrights in European shipyards, and along with Count Apraxin, his most trusted advisor, he encouraged foreign sailors to enter Russian service, thus beginning the Russian Navy. He pulled teeth to learn about medicine and gave medical lectures with the heads of those unfortunate enough to get themselves decapitated by displeasing him. He conceived the Russian Academy of Science, which was really started by his widow, Catherine, after his death, and brought European scientists to Russia. He founded St. Petersburg as well, killing, it has been said, 200,000 serfs to build it, and moved the capital there from its ancient site in Moscow, where the grim crenelated walls of the Kremlin stood above the Moscow River and the flat north-German plain. He apparently wanted to underline the change he was thrusting upon Russia, for the Kremlin was too steeped in the past and bore the marks of too many defeats; the city that had begun as a small palisaded village in the twelfth century had been over-run innumerable times by Mongols, Tatars, Turks, Poles, Swedes, French, Germans and rebellious factions of the Russian aristocracy. It had seen invasions, pillage and every conceivable violence, and the barbarous and bloody careers of Ivan the Great and Ivan the Terrible. It had burned down numerous times and been re-built; there were 1500 churches in it, with their bright-colored onion domes and a veritable forest of gilded crosses, but splendid palaces were surrounded by the hovels of the poor and the streets were dark and narrow. Peter had disliked it ever since the days when he had had to use it as a sort of fort during the revolt of the Guard Regiments; and now that the ancient enemies who had overrun it were beaten and he had got the unification of Russia under way, he wanted to get away from it.

The things he had done had not been done easily, or by gentle persuasion; there hadn't been any soothing propaganda or a series of Five Year plans to ease the change. Peter had been too violent a man for that. It has been reported that he never got into bed sober after he became Czar, but other reports discount this and say that he leaned more toward casual encounters with women and had more bastards than Louis XIV of France; and an indication of his character may be gathered from the fact that he had one of the alleged lovers of his second wife, Catherine, beheaded, and made her keep the severed head thereafter in a jar of alcohol on the mantel in her boudoir. Determined to westernize his coun-

try, he went at the westernization pell-mell and knouted the country along with him. If anyone objected, and many did, he was
knouted, stretched on the rack, jailed, sent to Siberia or simply
liquidated. The gallows and the torture chambers were the order
of the day. Peter was a one-man revolution, swinging an ax, ter-
rorizing a medieval world into modernity, and stopped at nothing.
They invented a proverb for him: "Near the Czar, near death."

Men had long worn Oriental clothing and beards; they were
ordered out of both, and if they were reluctant to comply, their
clothes were torn off and their beards plucked out; they were
lucky to escape with their lives. Women were ordered out of their
Oriental seclusion. A new society was established by ukase, and
there was a great upheaval and change in all social life. The idea
that everyone owed service to the state, a hangover from the two-
hundred-year Mongol occupation in the thirteenth and fourteenth
centuries, was intensified; serfs fell deeper into slavery, and nobles
gave more of their time to the army or the administration of the
country. Travel abroad was frowned upon; the power of the
Orthodox Church was more or less broken, and the Church was
made, to all intents, a department of the state; Peter declared himself Patriarch, his drinking companions were given titles that
made a mockery of the old order, and drunken parodies of ancient
rituals were held at court.

By 1718, when Peter returned from his trip to Europe, the
cowering empire was sufficiently under control to give him a
breathing space to think of the North Pacific, the short cut to
China and the request of the French Academy. He had been sending Swedish prisoners of war to the eastern coast of Siberia to
instruct the natives and their Cossack overlords in shipbuilding
and map making, and he decided to act. He sent two officers off to

Kamchatka to sail around the Kuriles and into the Pacific to find out whether Asia and America were joined. At least, that was the published reason. It has been said that they were really sent to search for an island in the Kuriles where the Japanese mined a precious white metal—probably silver. The officers got themselves to Kamchatka, on which there were several primitive posts guarded by Cossacks, sailed about the Kuriles for a time, and returned to St. Petersburg in 1722 or 1723. They made a verbal report to Peter, and that was all. It seems obvious that they didn't get very far into the Pacific; their trip was a disappointment, and convinced Peter that something more elaborate was needed in the way of an expedition if he was to find out anything.

The Treaty of Nystad, marking the final victory over the Swedes, had been signed by that time; Peter was a little more popular because he had beaten the old and troublesome enemy, but his health had begun to fail. The vitality that had made a shambles of the old order was rapidly leaving him, ruined more by his excesses than by his struggles to build a united nation. He knew that he was going to die, and concentrated all his failing strength upon getting the orders for an expedition to the Pacific written, and on December 23, 1724 (the Old Style Russian calendar, eleven days behind ours, will be used in this book), he had them finished. They read:

1- To find surveyors who have been to Siberia and returned.

2- To find among the naval lieutenants or sub-lieutenants such as could be sent to Siberia and Kamchatka.

3- To find among the apprentices or assistant master builders one who can build there a deck ship along the lines of the big ships here. For that purpose there should be sent with him young ship carpenters, and such instruments as may be needed, one quartermaster and eight sailors.

4- Likewise forward from here two sets of sails, blocks, cables and such like; four falconnets with the necessary ammunition; and one or two sailmakers.

5- If there be no such navigators in our Navy, a letter should be dispatched at once to Holland that two men be sent who know the sea in the north and as far as Japan. These men should come by Admiralty post.

The reports from the Senate and the Admiralty Council in relpy to these orders named nine such surveyors, three lieutenants and two sub-lieutenants. They recommended as commander a Captain Vitus Bering, a Dane in the Russian Navy known to Peter, or a man named Fonverd, and Fedor Koslov as shipbuilder. They noted that two sets of sails and the rigging for them would be sent, and added that there were several adequate navigators in the Russian Navy.

Peter selected Bering as commander, another Dane, named Martin Spanberg, and a Russian named Aleksey Chirikov as lieutenants, and a Russian named Peter Chaplin as sub-lieutenant. He then issued a ukase to the exiled Prince Dolgorukov, the governor of East Siberia, at Yakutsk, but it was Catherine who signed it:

We are sending to Siberia Fleet-Captain Vitus Bering with assistants to undertake a naval expedition and carry out such orders as he has from us. When he comes to you and asks for help of one kind or another you are to give it to him.

To complete the arrangements, Peter drew up and signed his instructions to Bering, but he didn't give them to Bering himself. He was so ill by that time that he had to leave this to Count Apraxin. He died on January 28, 1725, of urinary obstruction, probably from an old gonorrheal infection, and infection of the bladder, kidneys and accessory organs, but his death didn't disturb the arrangements. The vanguard of the Expedition, consisting of twenty-six men and twenty-four sleds piled with gear, had already pulled out of St. Petersburg on the twenty-fourth and were on their way to the peninsula of Kamchatka, the edge of the known world, 6000 miles or so across European Russia and the desolation of Siberia.

The men who were going a third of the distance around the world on that parallel of longitude before they would build a ship and search an unknown ocean were coarse and simple fellows, fantastically enduring, as Russian peasants have always been, who would get falling-down drunk when they could and bargain for native women if they had anything to bargain with or could steal it, for they would seldom get their pay. In summer they would stink from the accumulated sweat of weeks at the sweeps of clumsy river barges often stuck in bogs or on sand bars, be well smoked by their fires, greased by their cookery and devoured by unbelievable swarms of bloodsucking insects. At least a third of their way would be over land permanently frozen, with snow cover that lasts 200 to 220 days of the year; they would be half frozen all winter long and in autumn be chilled to the bone by working up to their necks in icy rivers to lift their clumsy barges over shoals and rapids, for the conventional way to get across Siberia was to use the river systems of the country. The big rivers—Ob, Yenisei, Lena, Indigirka and Kolyma—all rose in the south, wandered about, and finally emptied into the Arctic Ocean; they and their tributaries drained tremendous areas, and whatever trade moved in Siberia followed them, moving overland from one to the other.

These men, already started on their long struggle to move the

1

anchors, cannon, ship's blocks and other clumsy gear across one of the coldest, emptiest and most desolate parts of the earth, had some ill-defined idea of the difficulties of their way, but they were too inexperienced to have more than that. They knew they would be hungry and cold and that if they were hurt they would have to heal themselves or bear what injuries came to them. They accepted these things with typical Russian fatalism; they had been hungry and cold at home, most of them, and were well acquainted with the fact that the life of a poor man under the Czars was no bed of roses.

They had possibly heard of Kamchatka, as they had possibly heard of Mars, and were not curious about it. Getting to that far and nebulous place was all in a day's work, a matter of following orders, something decided upon by the Czar who they heard was dead and buried with staggering pomp and ceremony in the cold and gloomy city they had lately left. They didn't know or care that their little expedition was to be the forerunner of another that would be the greatest the world had ever seen, that ten long years would go by before they both were over, and that the cost of them would run over a million rubles—a fantastic amount of money in the exchange of that time—and at the end of it all most of them would be dead in seas where strange beasts moved about among wild storms and fogs that hid for weeks on end the new world and the sun.

chapter
two

WHILE THE GEAR to build and fit out the Expedition's ship in
Kamchatka moved toward the other side of the world, Vitus Jonas-
sen Bering, the man whom Peter had selected to command the
enterprise, waited in St. Petersburg for his orders. He was forty-
four years old, a tall Dane with dark eyes and hair who had been
born in Horsens, a seacoast town in Jutland. He was rather stout,
heavier now than he had been on the day, twenty-two years before, when Admiral Cruys, the Norse admiral of Peter's navy, had
talked to him in Amsterdam and offered him a job as sub-lieutenant in the new Russian fleet. The fleet sorely needed men who
knew the sea, and Cruys had interviewed a great many of them;
most of them had impressed him as barflies who wanted to strike
it rich in Russia with as little work as possible, but this round-
faced, serious young man, obviously poor, in a somewhat thread-
bare mate's coat, didn't. He was just back from a voyage to the
East Indies and there was a feeling of competence and purpose
about him despite his self-consciousness in the resplendent pres-
ence of an admiral. Cruys felt that he was honest and dependable;
he took an immediate liking to the boy, and a friendship sprang
up between the two sailors that was to last a long time. The new

sub-lieutenant could hardly have found a better man to take an interest in him. Cruys has been given most of the credit for putting the Russian Navy on the sea, and he had the ear of the Czar; he was one of the few people in St. Petersburg who entertained the Czar in his own house. He was vice president of the Council of the Admiralty, a full admiral after the Peace of Nystad, and well liked in the Scandinavian colony in St. Petersburg.

Bering had come of a good family; his mother's people had been ministers and judicial officers for two centuries, but his father had been poor and had many children; the boy had gone to sea in his teens to help out. He had an uncle, a brother of his mother's, named Vitus Bering, who was widely known and respected as a geographer, and when he left home, the boy had taken his uncle's name.

He was intelligent and eager for knowledge, always zealous to do his duty, and considerate of the men under him. He was first assigned to the Baltic Fleet and presently had the reputation of being a cheerful and capable officer and was steadily promoted. In 1718 he married one of the three pretty daughters of Matthias Pullse, a Viborg merchant. The girl was almost his direct opposite, for while he was thoughtful and rather deliberate, she was gay, somewhat flighty, fond of parties and the lively life of the capital. One of her sisters married a commissioner of state named Anton Selzer and the other married Vice Admiral Thomas Sanders, who for some reason took a dislike to Bering and maneuvered against him at court. Despite this, Bering was a captain of the second rank by 1720. He had charge of a number of important transport operations in the Swedish War, which he performed so capably that he came to Peter's attention; and so, after the Peace of Nystad was signed and promotions were being widely given out, he had expected to be made captain of the first rank. The promotion didn't come through. Sanders and Apraxin (who thought him not energetic enough and too inclined to be lenient in his discipline at a time when harshness was the order of the day) managed to get it withheld. Bering knew that he deserved promotion; he had done his work capably and well, and he was considerably depressed at being left dangling by people who had little reason except malice to move against him. By 1724 he'd had enough of it and asked for either promotion or discharge, and could get neither. Cruys, apparently, could do nothing for him at the time and Apraxin, who was managing a great number of things for the ailing Czar, refused to sign either the promotion or the discharge.

There was nothing he could do in such a situation, after twenty years' service; he sent in his papers and went home to a small estate he had bought in Sweden. His friends were outraged at the treatment that had been given him, and finally got word of it to the Czar. Peter still thought well of Cruys and his judgment, and recalled Bering's handling of the transport operations in the Swedish War; the Expedition, with its long march to the Pacific, needed such a man. Peter notified Apraxin that Bering was to be reinstated and promoted. Bering was recalled from Sweden, and several months later was put in charge of the Expedition.

It was extremely pleasant to be back in service again, to have the promotion that was due him, and to be put in charge of the Czar's last important project; and he wouldn't have been human if he didn't get a good deal of quiet satisfaction from the comeuppance administered to the coterie which had given him trouble. He was made much of by his friends, for they had won for him, and he avoided his brother-in-law. He didn't like courtiers, being an honest and unassuming man, too fair-minded and deliberate in his ways to understand them, and he was excited by the chance to make a name for himself in unknown seas while his brother officers eased off into the uneventful days of the peacetime navy. Probably he was also glad of the chance to get beyond reach of his detractors for a while, and away from the capital, where all sorts of subterranean maneuverings were going on. Catherine had ascended the throne, and was somewhat of an unknown quantity to whom Bering's record, and possibly his friends, meant little or nothing. He had heard of her that she had been a washerwoman, a trollop handed up through the army until Peter took her as his second wife without bothering to divorce his first; report made of her a short and huddled creature without looks or dignity who decorated herself with so much tasteless jewelry that she jangled when she walked. To balance this, in her favor, were other reports that she could nearly match the Czar in strength, that she went on difficult trips and even military campaigns with him, had borne him twelve children and often stood between his murderous rages and the Russian people. He knew, from the gossip, that the Senate was busily engaged in taking away from her some of the absolute power that Peter had held, and that the courtiers were even more busily maneuvering for more favorable positions for themselves and their friends.

He was glad that he would be out of it, or hoped that he would. His excitement was colored by uncertainty, for although the Admiralty College had sent off the gear, his own orders seemed to be a long time getting to him. Catherine or Apraxin might still suddenly decide to halt the supply train wherever it was and cancel the entire Expedition. He found it difficult to wait, and in order to keep busy and learn something about the history, general conditions and geography of Siberia, he visited the Siberia Office in Moscow and talked to anyone he could find who knew something about the place.

He found that little was really known of Siberia beyond the route along the rivers and the government posts that were scattered along them where all the trade moved. Most of the early exploration had been done by *promyshleniki* and the ever-restless Cossacks, who were allowed freedom of movement and a certain amount of autonomy in return for allegiance to the Crown. The Cossacks had got to the mouth of the Yenisei River, on the Arctic Ocean, early in the seventeenth century, after having fought pitched battles with Samoyedes, Ostyaks and Tunguses, the native tribes of those parts. They had fanned out from the Yenisei and discovered the Lena in 1630, and their exploration of this great river had inspired them to renewed activity. A Cossack named Staduchin found the Kolyma, the last large river to the east, and the fortified post of Nizhne-Kolymsk was established about seventy miles from its mouth. It was a thousand miles from Yakutsk, the capital of East Siberia, and remained a focal point for further explorations for one hundred years or so. Staduchin was also the first man to find the Chukchi, the redoubtable people of the eastern Arctic tundra; and it was from Nizhne-Kolymsk that Deshneff had gone on his voyage, and discovered the Anadyr. After Yakutsk had been established as a palisaded town, the Cossacks had moved east again until they came to the Sea of Okhotsk, where they built the town of Okhotsk; from Okhotsk they crossed the sea and conquered Kamchatka.

Bering had, of course, encountered Cossacks numerous times; it was impossible to move anywhere in Russia without encountering them and hearing about them; but he had never quite realized before what an extraordinary people they were. Their origin was obscure; their name came from a Turkish word meaning "wanderer," and the more he heard of their free-wheeling explorations and battles off in the blue a thousand miles from their bases, the more he was impressed by their hardihood and reckless spirit. They had probably come from Turkey or even farther south, as had a number of Siberian tribes—many of whom had legends stretching back into the mists of time of hot countries, lions and huge snakes.

Of the country itself he heard less, but enough to know of the endless blank spaces it contained. There were intimations—from travelers, not the Siberia Office—of drunkenness, lies, slander and thieving bureaucrats who victimized everyone, even more than they did in Russia itself. It all made traveling and transport sound difficult in the extreme, but about that he would have to find out for himself.

Back in St. Petersburg again, he spent what time he could with his wife and baby daughter and completed what planning he could with his senior lieutenant, Martin Spanberg. Spanberg was in the tradition of the tough, bucko mates who so often appear in the literature of the sea. He had been born in Jerne in 1698 and appears first as a lieutenant of the fourth class in the Russian Navy in 1720 commanding the packet boat that ran between Lubeck and Kronstadt, the harbor and naval base of St. Petersburg. He was an overbearing, heavy-fisted man who had the reputation of being coarse, cruel and vociferous, greedy and without culture; but he was also an excellent practical seaman, impetuous and active. He spoke very bad Russian, which he didn't bother to improve, and, properly controlled, would be a good man to have along. The junior lieutenant, a good and sensible Russian seaman named Aleksey Chirikov, and the young Russian sub-lieutenant Peter Chaplin had both gone forward with the gear, and Bering would have to get better acquainted with them later.

Both Bering and Spanberg were growing increasingly nervous about the fate of their Expedition, but on February 5 Count Apraxin, acting for Catherine, appeared and, with an ill grace, handed Bering his orders. They read:

1- Build in Kamchatka or in some other place in that region one or two decked boats.
2- Sail on these boats along the shore which bears northerly and (since its limits are unknown) seems to be part of America.
3- Determine where it joins America, or some settlement under European jurisdiction; if you meet a European ship learn from it the name of the coast and put it down in writing, make a landing to obtain more detailed information, draw up a chart and come back here.

The Admiralty had added that he was to levy on the Governor at Tobolsk, the capital of the Siberian province nearest to Russia, for mechanics and supplies, and make a monthly report to the Admiralty College.

Bering said a long good-by to his family, and with Spanberg and the remaining five men of his company he left St. Petersburg the same day. It was the coldest and foggiest month of the year, but traveling wasn't too difficult yet. There were roads, even if they were bad ones, and post houses, occasional towns such as Vologda, Veliki Ustyug, Kai, places that grew increasingly smaller and more primitive until they became small and infrequent villages of a few thatched wooden houses on each side of the road. The travelers could still be comparatively comfortable in the Russian winter in these places and at the government posts they came to. They got to the Urals and through them early enough so that they didn't have to contend with the spring floods near the mountains.

Once past the Urals they were in Siberia, skirting the great marshes and sphagnum bogs and open swampy spruce forests with which they would have to deal for nearly a thousand miles. Traveling began to grow rougher. Siberia was divided into provinces, each controlled by a voivode, or governor, appointed by the Siberia Office in Moscow for terms of two years or more. It was very difficult to get good men to go into such a dangerous and uncomfortable country; and as Moscow was as yet not appreciative of the possibilities of Siberia, and interested primarily in the revenue that could be wrung out of it, it was glad to take what men it could get. What it got was just what one would expect in the circumstances: a bad lot, interested only in making itself, its family and the friends it had brought along rich, or exiles who were bitter men longing for home.

The opportunities were there for thievery, for the governors were in the main the court of last resort for the inhabitants, and all fines, fees, licenses, duties and the tribute laid on the rich fur trade—which was the only industry in East Siberia—passed through their hands. Of all the provincial income the tribute was the richest; for when one considers that in 1670 the voivode of Yakutsk's records show 18,450 sable, 6284 red fox and a number of other skins to be the official talley, with the true take impossible to come by and possibly double these numbers, it can be seen that the pickings were considerable. All skins had to be sold to Russians, and the Russian traders who managed to survive had to pay license, import and export duties, trumped-up fines, fees and tolls, and were searched and robbed at every opportunity. The natives,

who were assessed at a fixed rate despite population fluctuations
from smallpox, tuberculosis and venereal disease bestowed upon
them by their conquerors and the accidents of life in a cold climate,
were robbed more thoroughly. They had to produce skins or buy
them in the open market, and if they had no money to do this
they were jailed; if they revolted or refused they were killed and
their women handed over to the Cossacks. They suffered woefully
at the hands of the understrappers, who had the unfortunate example of their superiors always before them; and many natives
were robbed of their tribute at one place and then asked for it
later somewhere else, so that many of them paid it several times a
year.

All of the supplies and wages for the bureaucracy also passed
through the hands of the voivodes, and strange things happened
to it. All in all, things became so bad, and the universal thievery
so expensive to Moscow, that special customs officers, called
golovas, were appointed to keep a check on the voivodes. In most
cases the voivode and the golova joined forces and sent the profits
of their collaboration back to Russia by their families or friends,
or sold their stolen furs in China.

It does not require much stretch of the imagination to come at
the moral climate of all Siberia; and East Siberia, east of the Lena
River, which had only been conquered in the sixteenth century,
being furthest from Moscow, was the worst of all. It was a land
of venal and degraded men, slander and drunkenness; a number
of officials were exiles and not at all happy about it; in its desolate
reaches bands of criminals and disaffected men roved about, and
to the north and east lived the unconquered and warlike Chukchi
and Koryaks. Even in the provincial seats women and girls were
bought and sold, with the approval of the government so long as

35

a tax was paid on the transactions; natives were drafted for the hard work, usually at a time when they could least afford it; and, as "the Czar was far away," the Imperial orders and ukases often received rather scant attention. It was always easier to bring scurrilous charges against a man at the capital than to go to a lot of work and comply with his instructions or the instructions issued to help him. Besides, there never was a surplus of supplies; if the Expedition got them, there might be a scarcity before more came in or crops, if any, were ready to harvest the following year.

The worst of the officials and the difficulties of dealing with them were further along the way, however. Tobolsk, which had been founded by the Cossacks in 1587, was the first provincial capital the Expedition came to, and was too close to Russia proper to allow the officials much leeway. It was, as cities went in Siberia, an important place with a population of about 10,000 people; travelers to the east fitted out there. The Metropolitan of the Orthodox Church had his big stone palace within the palisaded walls of the fortress high above the river; but a good part of the town, built mostly of wood, was lower down on the river flats and was frequently flooded.

Bering and his little party reached Tobolsk on March 16, joining Chirikov, Chaplin and the twenty-six men who had left St. Petersburg before them with the gear. The weather had turned much colder, making traveling too difficult; they weren't hardened to it yet, and holed up until the middle of May. Bering requisitioned supplies, added thirty-four more men to his party and, when the ice broke up, took to the Irtysh River in seven rafts and four keel-less, flat-bottomed boats and started down the river with the current for Samarovsk, where the Irtysh joined the Ob. These boats, called *doshcheniki* in Siberia, were thirty-five to

forty feet long, carried a single sail, and were rowed and steered
by long two-man sweeps.

They, or others like them, were to be much in use for a great
deal of the remainder of the trip. Everyone with heavy material
to transport across the country used them, or smaller copies of
them. The Siberian river system, in which all the rivers eventually
flowed north into the Arctic Ocean, gave through the rivers themselves and their tributaries a sort of interconnected waterway that
ran more or less along the sixtieth parallel and could be used with
occasional portages almost to the Sea of Okhotsk.

It was an easier way to travel than overland, but still a great
deal of work, and the season when the rivers were free of ice was
not a very long one. The short trip to Samarovsk was the best of
it, for they were going with the current; after that, for a thousand
miles or so, they had to move upstream. Chaplin was sent ahead
with orders from the governor at Tobolsk to the people at
Yeniseisk and Ust Kut, where the Kut flowed into the Lena, to
build more boats by the time the Expedition appeared. The rest
of them got their backs into moving against the Ob.

The Ob is a big river, slow, meandering through a flat country
of great bogs of sphagnum moss and open spruce forests and
liable to change its course occasionally like most of the rivers of
western Siberia. The insects, mosquitoes and black flies, which
hatch in prodigious multitudes in such boggy country in spring,
hung over the men in clouds and sucked quarts of their blood.
There were difficulties until the spring floods subsided, for it
was all too easy to lose the main body of the stream and run
aground on high land or wander off into backwaters and be left
by the falling river; but they got to Narim, where they branched
off on to a tributary stream called the Ket. The Ket took them to

Makovaska Post, which had been built as a palisaded fort in 1619 against the Ostyaks, who had given the Cossacks trouble for a while.

From the post they had to move overland for several hundred miles, manhandling their clumsy gear across the bogs, to Yeniseisk —a place of five or six hundred wooden houses and a decaying wooden fort, occupied mostly by traders who spent a good deal of their time getting drunk and spreading venereal disease among the natives. At Yeniseisk, Bering added thirty carpenters and blacksmiths to the roster, where they got on the new boats built on Chaplin's orders to sail on the Yenisei and the Upper Tunguska. The terrible clouds of mosquitoes, black flies and gnats began to thin out, but there were other troubles. The Yenisei marks a sort of boundary between eastern and western Siberia; the land changes; the rivers no longer wander through swampy country but cut their way through pre-Cambrian rock and become swift and have many rapids in them. The Upper Tunguska was worse than the Yenisei; there were three long stretches of rapids on the Expedition's part of it, and a number of wide, rocky shoals, some of which were several miles long. The boats had to be fairly carried over them, and by now the bite of autumn was in the air, the larches were turning to feathery gold, and the water was cold. The men were in it a good deal of the time. The pine and larch forests grew gloomier and thicker on the banks; and when they came to the Ilim, the tributary that was to take them to Ilimsk, the flat-boats wouldn't go up at all: the river was too rocky and swift. Smaller boats were sent out from Ilimsk, under the direction of a Russian or two and rowed by Tunguses, the cheerful, horse-breeding natives of those parts, to take the heavier materials; the lighter stuff was left with guards to be sent for later, when there was snow on the ground.

Bering had wanted to go a hundred miles or so farther to Ust Kut, where they would get on to the Lena, but he was told that the place was too small to accommodate the entire party there for the winter. Further, the boats for which Chaplin had taken the orders ahead hadn't been built. They were, as Bering was finding out, getting far enough from Russia now so that distance took some of the authority from an Imperial ukase; and he suspected, quite correctly, that this state of affairs wasn't going to improve. The country was too wild, the winter would be too severe, and settlements were too scarce along the way to even think of getting to Yakutsk, the capital of Siberia. It was now the end of September, freeze-up time; there was nothing to do but spend the winter at Ilimsk.

It was a poor little village, small and primitive, a stopping place for traders, but there was food there; there was nothing else to do. To save time in the spring, Bering sent Spanberg (who was inclined to get into trouble when he hadn't enough to occupy him) with thirty-nine carpenters and laborers overland to Ust Kut to build fifteen barges during the winter. Chaplin, if he had followed orders, was already in Yakutsk, where he was to have more boats built and send off a force to Okhotsk to fell trees, prepare lumber and begin the construction of a ship or two to get the Expedition across the Sea of Okhotsk to the western coast of Kamchatka.

Although they had been on the way for nine months, a good deal of the time at the sweeps, things hadn't gone too badly. There had been troublesome days or weeks—in the spring, when rivers were flooded and some of the boats got away from the

39

rivers into the flooded lowlands and backwaters and were almost left there as the water went down; in the summer, with the almost unbearable plagues of insects; in the early fall, when they reached the swifter rivers and had the rapids to contend with— but all in all the transport operation had been a success. They still had their supplies and materials; they had lost very little of them, and the men, while they were worn down by the long weeks at the sweeps and their work in the cold water getting the boats through rapids and shoals, were in fair shape. The natives, who had done most of the heavier work, were in worse shape; but they were expendable.

So far, so good; but now Bering began to worry. There was a long, cold and idle winter in front of him; he had thirty or forty men, healthy and accustomed to hard work, who would presently be rested, in a cramped and primitive little village with nothing to do and no money to spend, surrounded by the endless dense and gloomy pine forests where a deathly stillness held the snowy world. Besides, they had covered the better-known part of their route; they were a long way from home, and the farther they went, the wilder and emptier the country became. The thousand miles or so to Yakutsk would not be too bad; the men would be moving with the Lena's current instead of against it; but no one in Ilimsk seemed to know much about the route from Yakutsk to Okhotsk. It was too far away.

Bering finally found out that the provincial governor at Irkutsk, several hundred miles to the south near cold and windy Lake Baikal, had formerly been governor at Yakutsk and was supposed to know the eastern country; so, during the winter he and Spanberg made a trip on horseback to see the man. The town, while not as big as Tobolsk, was important, because most of the trade with China moved through there. The country was fertile, food was cheap, and the houses were better than those in most Siberian towns. Besides the government buildings, there were churches with onion domes, monasteries, a good bazaar, a courthouse, a public bathhouse and even a functioning police force; but the syphilis rate was high and there was the usual drunkenness. Irkutsk had grown out of quarters established in 1652 by the tax gatherers. It was forty-five miles from Lake Baikal, on the Angora River, a tributary of the Yenisei; it seldom got very warm even in summer, being at an elevation of several thousand feet, but the climate was dry and pleasant.

The Governor, Mikhaelo Izmailov, was not particularly glad to see them; he had been ordered to get a supply of rye flour to Yakutsk for them by late spring, and flour was always scarce. However, he had his orders from St. Petersburg, and along with several Cossacks and a trader who was wintering with him he sat down and mapped out a route. From Yakutsk they were to go down the Lena to the Aldan, up the Aldan to the Yudoma, up the Yudoma to the head of navigation where someone had erected a cross. From there they would have to go overland to Okhotsk, Izmailov said with a sour grin, for he had no sympathy with the enterprise; the whole thing had been a nuisance to him and brought his own supplies a little low, and there would be empty bellies and much subdued grumbling until the new crop was in next fall. Bering took it from all this that the trip would not be an easy one, and as it turned out he was right. The only thing that Izmailov really warned them about was not to get too far north. The Chukchi, who lived there, were still beating any Cossack detachment sent against them and denying access to their country. They were hardy enough to kill the huge Siberian

41

and polar bears with spears, and although they cooked their meat—they ate little else—they ate it cold, and usually finished their meals with several big handsful of snow to keep their temperature comfortable. They were a murderous lot, supremely tough, self-sufficient and too proficient by far in a fight—a good people to stay far away from.

Doubtless, Izmailov concluded, there would be a sufficiency of guides at Yakutsk. Some of the Yakuts, who lived in that country, had been to Okhotsk; besides, all the traders and trappers in East Siberia, many of whom had also been to Okhotsk, came to Yakutsk during the summer for the fur trade. He took Bering's requisition for twenty blacksmiths and carpenters with an ill grace and sent him off, promising the grain and the people.

Later in the winter the carpenters and the blacksmiths and the rye flour appeared from Izmailov; the rest of the flour, to be furnished by the bureaucrats at Ilimsk, was rounded up; and as the idleness of his crew was beginning to cause some problems, Bering decided not to wait any longer. He got his company on the move and took them to Ust Kut, where Spanberg (a rough disciplinarian), the cold spring weather and the final work on the boats brought them back into line again. The Lena broke the ice in May, and the boats were loaded and started down the river. Chirikov was left to bring up the rear.

The Lena is one of the world's largest rivers; on the upper river, upon which the Expedition was moving, the banks are high, rocky and picturesque, and there are great forests of pine and larch; the right, or south, bank is more mountainous, and the best sables and other furs in Siberia came from there. The north bank was not so well forested, the soil was not very good, and the quality of the fur coming from there was poor. Most of the trapping was done close to the river; the south bank forests had not been very deeply penetrated at that time, and the boats passed occasional burned and desolate areas where careless hunters had set the forests on fire. There would soon be other people on the river: traders and merchants from the south who would start for Yakutsk and the north as soon as break-up would let them, bringing corn, meal, Circassian tobacco, tea, sugar, rum—anything that could be traded for the winter's catch of fur.

It was a little too early for the traders yet, but the Expedition would occasionally see Tunguses or Yakuts along the banks. Both tribes were trappers and breeders of the tough little Mongol horses; they looked like Tatars, which is what the Russians called the Mongols. The Tunguses had once held the country, but the Yakuts had come in and beaten them and driven many of them out. Now they lived more or less in peace together, but there were many more Yakuts than Tunguses; the Yakuts were the tougher of the two and didn't even like one another very much. They were unsocial and vindictive toward one another, although hospitable toward strangers. They were still in their winter yurts, which were made of thin boards in the shape of truncated pyramids and covered with branches and mud with a couple of windows made with sheets of ice, melting now in the warming weather. They would soon move to their summer houses, which were made of strips of boiled birchbark sewed together, with oiled fish membrane for windows, built over poles. These yurts were circular tents, and were moved around as the Yakuts looked for grass that could be cut and dried for hay; and as anyone who went into one soon found out, they stank beyond bearing. These people ate boiled horsemeat and drank mare's milk; they loved fat and ate it raw, melted, fresh or spoiled, and grated the inner bark of the larch and mixed it with fat, fish and milk to make a soup which they drank in incredible quantities.

They were a rugged people, superstitious and gloomier than the cheerful Tunguses, and good men with horses; they could endure terrible cold and hunger; they knew how to survive in an extraordinarily difficult climate.

Along the river the larches took on their tender spring green and darkened, the sky grew lively with long strings of ducks and geese headed north, and the foliage along the banks burgeoned toward the summer, toward the blossoming of dark iris, spirea, wild rose and lilies. A little musk deer occasionally would be seen and once in a while a moose along the sand bars or the banks of the river.

The Expedition made good time, helping the Lena's current with the sails and sweeps; when the wind came up against them, they used an ingenious device common along the river: the watersail. This device was made of four larch trunks nearly as long as the boats, lashed together, weighted with stones and sunk six feet or so lengthwise under the boats. The current acted upon it and carried the boats against the wind.

A little after the middle of June they reached Yakutsk, the capital of Siberia, on its barren flat near the river. The town, which is one of the coldest in the world, was as bleak as it was possible for a town to be. It centered around an old palisaded fort built by the Cossacks in 1647; there were a few decent buildings, but most of the five or six hundred structures comprising the town were very mean and primitive. It was a gloomy and somber place, where the winter temperatures sometimes went down to seventy-two degrees below zero, and in the height of summer occasionally reached one hundred degrees. There wasn't much social life except eating, drinking and singing; the favorite drink of the town was made of brandy, berries and sugar, and the Russians who had children had Yakut nurses for them, so that the children spoke better Yakut than Russian.

Yakutsk was the trading center of all East Siberia, and fur from the surrounding country, walrus ivory and mammoth tusks and bones from the Chukchi country, the far north, came from there. Some of the bones probably found their way into the Chinese pharmacopoeia, powdered as dragon bones, a sovereign medicine; but it was the tusks that were important. These mammoth tusks, which were larger than those of any elephant living now, gave the Chinese the great preponderance of the ivory they carved. The tusks had been drifting down from the northeast of Siberia since before the birth of Christ. They were found in unbelievable numbers; records show that almost 50,000 of them have found their way into China in the past two or three hundred years. There was an annual trade fair in the town in summer; merchants came down the Lena after break-up with Circassian tobacco, brandy, rum, tea, sugar, Chinese cotton goods, hardware and glass to trade with the Russians for the furs and ivory they had traded all year from the natives, and with the natives for what furs they had managed to keep for themselves after the tax gatherers got through with them. Early August was the best time to move about on the river; by early September the river and the extensive morasses of the country began to feeeze hard again.

From what Bering had learned from Izmailov at Irkutsk and from the talk around Yakutsk, he knew that the worst part of the trip was ahead of him. Most of the country was practically unknown, there were no trails or roads, the country was composed of more or less parallel ridges with lakes and swamps between them, and there were swift rivers along the way which would have to be crossed somehow. He decided to send Spanberg on with thirteen boats and two hundred men to transport the heaviest and most unmanageable material by water. Spanberg was to sail down the Lena to the Aldan, up the Aldan to the Yudoma and on to Yudoma Cross, the head of navigation. Bering himself and a few men, with Yakuts to help, would go overland by horseback to Okhotsk, carrying the lighter supplies. He called on the provincial governor for natives to help on the barges, and asked him to round up about six hundred horses and hold them in readiness for the trip.

The governor was willing enough to supply the native labor. There were always more natives. But the horses and the hay to feed them was something else again; horses were valuable and hay was always scarce; the Yakuts worked themselves down to skin and bone to make enough of it during the short summers, and seldom had enough, and he and the natives would be run short for their winter supply. He struggled to scale down the exorbitant demands, but Bering was insistent. There was not even a refuge for the governor in that valuable tactic of officialdom the world over, protracted delay. The Russians of the town were after him to get the Expedition and its troublesome people out of the way, especially before the trade fair began; and Bering, on the heels of his other demands, now wanted enough hides to make 2000 leather sacks for his flour. It was impossible to conceive what would be wanted next.

Bering, on his part, had heard some things that whetted his appetite to be gone, and he kept a steady pressure on the governor.

He had talked to several wandering traders who had come into Yakutsk and they had told him of rumors farther north that there was a large country out in the Icy Sea (the Arctic Ocean off the northern shore of the continent) above the mouth of the Kolyma River. This sort of talk had been part of the gossip in East Siberia for a long time, but one had to be in East Siberia to hear it. No one in the Admiralty in St. Petersburg would have encountered it. There were no newspapers or magazines to spread local tales of this sort. It was like the Deshneff report, buried and lost in the provincial capital. This was exciting news, for it was very likely that the Expedition, if it got to East Cape and found no land connecting the Cape with America, would sail around to the Kolyma, where there was a Russian post; and if they got that far they could go a little farther and discover the new continent.

In addition, a nephew of the Cossack chief Shestakov appeared and joined the Expedition. Shestakov had been up near East Cape, fighting the wild Chukchi, and the nephew had been with him; and this nephew was not only full of rumors of a large country to the east of East Cape—a place closer than the Kolyma—but he had seen some of the prisoners the Chukchi had brought back from this country. They were not like Chukchi; they were probably Aleuts from beyond the Diomedes. There was no doubt that they had come from a strange and unknown place.

These things, this talk and rumor, were like a breath of fresh air to Bering, who for a year and a half had been like a man laboring in a closed room with his nose to the grindstone of the multifarious vexations of the transport operation. The everlasting swamps and rapids, the months at the sweeps, the bloodsucking insects of the summer and the cold and discomfort of the winter, the backbreaking toil of getting anchors, tackle, cannon and other

47

unwieldy and intractable objects across thousands of empty miles, and the troubles with supply and men who broke bones, suffered hideous injuries that had to heal themselves, or who often acted like stupid or contrary children had dimmed the enthusiasm of the start.

Now some of it returned, and Bering further increased his pressure on the governor. That unhappy man squirmed and pleaded and finally appealed to his superior, Prince Dolgurokov; but the Prince, with an Imperial ukase hanging over him, was powerless to do anything but shrug and turn away.

chapter
three

THE NATIVE HELP was rounded up and handed over to Spanberg, and he began loading for his trip down the Lena. He was leaving a little late in the year, and there was some head-shaking among people who knew the country; for when he got onto the Aldan and the Yudoma, the country grew higher and rougher, rising from the lowlands along the Lena. The valley of the Yudoma was comparatively narrow, running between mountains and rising to the plateau they had to cross to reach Okhotsk; both rivers would be swift, at least until they froze, there would be much colder weather, a good deal of snow, and no posts on the way to help him if he got into trouble. The route was over practically trackless wilderness; the narrow river beds were full of huge rocks and rounded boulders that crippled horses and broke men down, and the mountains were worse. The higher they grew, the more miry they became, and their tops held enormous quaking bogs; horses broke through them and couldn't be got out, and many firm-looking places on the trail, when stepped upon, caused the ground to shudder in terrifying waves for thirty yards in all directions.

None of the initiated worried about Spanberg himself. He had gone a long way toward building a reputation for reckless willfulness, and the natives had got to calling him Our Little Father Martin Petrovich Trump, in sardonic appreciation of his likeness to an autocratic and unanswerable Czar, and few questioned that he could survive almost anything; but he wasn't taking the trip by himself. Some of the people with him had managed to make a few friends, and the friends suspected that they were headed for trouble.

The few members of the Expedition who were left watched the thirteen barges, loaded with 204 people and all the freight that was too difficult to send overland on the horses, swing out into the current, move on downstream and finally disappear, and then turned to finishing their leather sacks. They finished them presently and filled them with flour—about twenty-six tons of it. There wasn't enough leather pack harness, so a sufficiency of rope was commandeered, scrounged or extemporized to piece it out, and the unwilling horses were loaded with 180 pounds each. Most of them hadn't been broken to packs; they were all fat and feeling good from the summer's grazing, and many of them bucked their packs off or got down and rolled on them. There were some spirited scenes in Yakutsk before the long line of horses were packed, resigned to their burdens and on their way. Chirikov was left to winter in Yakutsk and bring more flour in the spring.

They would have had a very rough time of it without the Yakuts who had been sent along, for the Yakuts were very good with horses; even with the Yakuts managing the animals, singing their endless gloomy songs and tying horsehair to trees to propitiate the spirits, things were difficult enough. At first the going was muddy; there were swamps between the low parallel ridges of the country they were going through, and bogged horses are all too liable to plunge brainlessly about and throw themselves or shake their loads loose, infecting their neighbors with the same notions. Presently, however, they got to the Yudoma and under the Verkhoyansk Range and began to climb it to reach the plateau, which ran nearly to Okhotsk; and as they had been even later in starting than Spanberg—toward the end of August—the weather began to get cold. They weren't very far south of one of the coldest localities in East Siberia, where winter temperatures of seventy degrees below zero weren't uncommon, and soon they began to get snow that covered up the grazing, which was already past its prime. Yakut horses were tough beasts, accustomed to hard lives, but they had to eat. There were too many of them together and there wasn't sufficient time to let them forage through the snow; no hay had been brought along for them. They lost their condition rapidly, and by the time the party got to Yudoma Cross, the horses were falling along the trail. Several tons of flour had to be left at Yudoma Cross; loads were increased on the remaining horses and word was passed to pick up the pace. A short early blizzard gave them an intimation of what the country could do, and they wanted to get off the windy plateau with its great areas of quaking, apparently bottomless bogs, its 2000-foot elevation and scattered peaks that ran up to 4200 feet.

It grew colder and the wind wailed a more biting song, but it was impossible to get more out of the faltering horses or to hurry the Yakuts. They were quite casual about the weather. They had an enviable reputation of being the iron men of East Siberia, a land of rugged characters. Bering had been told in Yakutsk how these extraordinary people, whose origins were lost in antiquity, could sleep in the snow at temperatures of fifty below zero with nothing over them but the light fur jackets they wore all day. They would first warm themselves by the campfire, put little

51

pieces of fur in their nostrils and ears, cover their faces with a cloth arranged with a small opening for air, stretch out and snore away until morning, when they would be discovered near the burnt-out fire, well furred with a thick coat of rime. It seemed impossible that any human being could stand exposure of this sort, but the Yakuts stood it as a matter of course. They had a metabolism that no doctor in these days would subscribe to. The chilly autumn weather meant little to them.

When they finally dropped down off the plateau to Okhotsk, worn thin and tired out, they found only ten small Russian houses that were no better than huts in the town. It was three miles from the river where Chaplin and his crew had been building the ship to take them across the Sea of Okhotsk, and there was no accommodation whatever for the party that Bering had with him, much less for the crowd that would be coming in with Spanberg sooner or later. Chaplin's crew had been sleeping on the uncompleted ship, and about filled it; there was nothing for the weary party to do but set to work and build shelter for themselves and warehouses for the supplies they had brought.

Chaplin was well dressed down for not anticipating this contingency, although his orders had contained nothing about it; no one had thought of the matter at the time. The carpenters were pulled off their unfinished work on the ship and added to Bering's party, and the construction began. It was cold and grinding work. There wasn't any timber close to hand; it had to be felled and dressed several miles away and carried into Okhotsk on the men's backs, for the horses that had survived the trip, thinned down by starvation and exposure, were dying every day. It was too late in the season to cut hay for them; there was nothing to do but let them die.

When the huts and warehouses were finished, the carpenters were sent back to the ship and the crew were put to work catching fish and making salt for them and for the beef that was supposed to be driven in the spring. Whether it would appear or not was a question that time would answer, but they had to be ready for it. The fishing was a cold, wet and not very productive affair at that time of year; spring and summer was when the big runs of fish took place, but Bering insisted upon it. He was as tired as the rest of them, and not very reasonable. Fishing seemed like futile, punishing nonsense to the exhausted men; they all wanted to sit resting around the fires under the salt kettles and pour in a bucket of sea water once in a while. Incipient mutiny was in the air; several of the men were beaten, and the rest were threatened with action by the Cossacks around Okhotsk. It was a bad time, dragging itself out during the winter weather in surly, covert disobedience which severely tried Bering's habit of consideration of his crew. He had more than this on his mind, for he hadn't heard from Spanberg and did not know what was happening to him.

He found out during a short, gloomy day in late December. Two men, much the worse for wear, appeared with the news that the senior lieutenant had been frozen in with his boats on the Derbi River, a tributary of the Yudoma near the point where it flowed into the Aldan. Many of the Yakuts, with whom he had been very high-handed, had simply disappeared and left him shorthanded. He had made 100 hand sleds upon which to haul as much as he could. It had taken him too long to move against the current of the Aldan, with his late start and the unusually early descent of winter, and his provisions had been used up in the ruin of his schedule or stolen by the natives. The snow had been heavy and further delayed him, and things had gone from bad to worse. Hunger caught up with him; the men had been reduced to eating some of their leather clothes and their boots. They had finally got to Bering's trail, and began to eat the dead and frozen horses that were little more than skin and bone, the two men said, and when they had finally got to Yudoma Cross and found the flour Bering had been forced to leave there it was as though God had finally taken mercy on them. The flour was the only thing that had enabled them to survive.

By the famished and beaten look of the two men, their description of Spanberg and his party hungry and cold in the wild and trackless valley of the Yudoma, trying to get on with hand sleds in six feet of snow on a diet of starved and frozen horses, it was obvious that they needed all the help they could get. It took from eight to ten weeks in winter to go from Okhotsk to Yakutsk if anybody was foolish enough to try it; Spanberg wasn't that far, but he was far enough. It was almost January now, the middle of winter, a time when people stayed home and avoided the bitter cold and killing blizzards of the plateau, but something had to be done. Bering got together a party composed of a few of his men, some of the Yakuts who had come with him, and natives drafted from around Okhotsk; dog teams were organized, supplies gathered together, and the men were told to go out and find the lieutenant.

The incipient mutiny that had been smoldering for weeks burst into flame; the party refused to go. They had been overworked for too long, they said; they were played out, they hadn't received their pay and the weather was murderous. Everything they said was true. Bering tried to reason with them and got no-

54

where; he hardly expected to. With great reluctance and a good deal of hope he gave orders for some gallows to be built in the snow, and let it be known that the families of the men who would be hanged would be turned over to the Cossacks. That broke the revolt and the relief party took the trail, vanishing into the icy plateau with its trailing birch and thickets of scrubby Dahurian larch. An anxious time of waiting began for Bering, who was left to wonder how many of the men he had sent out would get back again, and whether he would ever see Spanberg and his crew.

They stumbled into Okhotsk around the middle of January, but not all of them. Many of the natives had died on the way; some who returned were so used up by the trip that they died after they got back. Some had deserted and, as Bering discovered later, went back to Yakutsk and preferred charges of cruelty against him. They had contended with snow up to seven feet deep or more in places, and at night had had to dig down through it to the ground to sleep. The Russians, the crewmen, were frost-bitten, done up, down to their last reserves. In the freezing nights, in their hungry holes in the snow with the aurora flaring over them in the sky, they had had a lot of time to think of their homes and the two years they had been away from them, the long miles they had come and the unguessable time and distance they still had to go. They weren't like the fur hunters, the *promyshleniki* or the Cossacks, adventurers like the mountain men of the American west who loved the wandering, rootless life with its iron hardships and its dangers and kept on going in the hope of a fight or to see what was over the next hill. Their lives at home had held little pleasure or hope, but they wished with all their hearts that they were home again.

They had been unable to bring any of the supplies back with them; these were scattered along the trail at four or five places, guarded from bears, wolves and wandering natives by several unfortunates who had had rough and hasty shelters knocked together for them and been left some food. They held their comfortless vigils until the middle of February, when Spanberg, who had recuperated enough to set out from Okhotsk with ninety men and what dog teams could be gathered together, reached them again. The weather was no better, and to transport the Expedition's most difficult material on sleds in six feet of snow was a terrible undertaking; but at least the men were fed this time, and Spanberg, still in a simmering rage when he thought of the deserting natives before, showed little mercy to them or to himself. He returned to Okhotsk early in April, ahead of his crew, which got back about the middle of the month; they left enough so that another trip had to be made with horses around the end of April. What they failed to bring in was sent back to Yakutsk with the men who had been detailed to watch the stuff over the winter, and they were told to get receipts for it; further, they were to hold out what iron and tar they could transport and fetch these things to Kamchatka in 1728 without too much tarrying. They must have wondered, if they had that much ability to wonder left in them, where sweet reason came into such a roundabout business.

Bering had always been a considerate man, but here he was not considerate. He seems to have lost his balance a little. Of a certainty the two years had been hard on him; the Ministry of Marine, to whom he was supposed to report monthly, had sat comfortably in the capital and bedeviled him with complaints of slowness and mismanagement, and he had got little support from anybody. He had been hungry, cold, overworked, frustrated and put upon, and it all had its effect upon him. He wasn't the sort to shrug all this off, and he had no idea that his best days were behind him. He would never quite get back to his old self again, and harder and harder times were in store for him.

The ship, christened *Fortune*, was finished in June, loaded with most of the materials on hand and sent off to Kamchatka under the command of Spanberg. He was to unload at the mouth of the Bolshaya River, on the west coast, send off the carpenters he had taken with him to the Lower Kamchatka Post on the east coast to prepare ship timbers from the fine larch forests there and return. By the time he got back, Chirikov had come in from Yakutsk with forty or fifty tons of additional flour. This was loaded on *Fortune*, and between that ship and *Lodiya*, an old boat used by the tribute collectors, the entire party and what was left of the supplies were embarked on August 21.

They made the mouth of the Bolshaya without incident; but as the western coast of Kamchatka is flat and marshy and the coastal waters shallow, the two ships had to drop anchor three miles off shore and everything had to be carried in by small boats. There was a Russian post there called Bolsheretsk, a mean little place of fourteen Russian houses. It had been founded in 1702, burned in 1707 during the revolt of the Kamchadals and rebuilt in 1711, and was still a stockaded post mostly composed of government buildings and a vodka distillery. It was usually garrisoned by about forty Cossacks. It took them nearly a month to get the cargo from the ships into town. The heavier materials were again loaded into small boats and sent up the Bystraya River, toward the Lower Kamchatka Post on the east coast. The Bystraya, a tributary of the Bolshaya, was a smallish river with a swift current, full of rapids and shoals. It would be grueling work all the way, and when they reached the head of navigation they still had about eighty miles to go over the spine of the country to the Lower Kamchatka Post. They didn't make it. Finally the material had to be brought back and carried along with the rest of the Expedition.

The rest of the Expedition made itself more or less at home in Bolsheretsk until the onset of winter, and then started out with the dog teams to get themselves to that part of the Pacific which is now called Bering Sea. Once again, natives—Kamchadals this time—were pressed into service. Their destination was the Lower Kamchatka Post.

This last leg of the trip was far from simple. Kamchatka is a peninsula, 700 miles or so in length and 250 miles wide at its widest point. There are two mountain ranges. The main, or western, range runs down the middle of it; the coast range, on the east, is intermittent and not very long. The elevation of the main range is around 4000 feet. The coast range runs around 4700, but there are a number of active volcanoes on it and the highest, Klyuchevskaya, goes up to an elevation of 11,830 feet and sends a column of smoke and ashes over a mile above its summit. Between the ranges runs the Kamchatka River, which finally swings to the east around Klyuchevskaya and flows into the Bering Sea. Its valley is fairly flat; most of it is tundra, and in the summer this tundra is swampy and difficult to move about in. In winter the temperature in the river valley drops as low as fifty degrees below zero and there are terrible storms, called *poorgas*, which sweep down from the higher country and bring clouds of sleet and snow which move across the land like smoke, blotting out everything and catching the unwary traveler away from shelter to snow him under and freeze him to death.

There were three Russian posts on Kamchatka: Bolsheretsk, on the west coast; Upper Kamchatka Post, in the middle of the peninsula on the Kamchatka River; Lower Kamchatka Post, near the mouth of the river to the north. This is a confusing contradiction in terms, for in reality the Lower Post was far to the north of the Upper Post.

When Bering left Bolsheretsk he had to go over a pass in the main range, drop down to the river valley to Upper Post, and follow the river to Lower Post on the Bering Sea. This was a trip of between 300 and 400 miles, most of it over the tundra of the river valley. The river was navigable to small boats for the last 200 miles, but the boats had to be built after the river was reached, and Bering decided that it was impractical to build the large number of boats he would need in the middle of the swampy tundra country. He decided instead to dare the winter, using dog teams to haul his materials.

On the face of it, it would have made more sense if he had gone around the southern point of Kamchatka during the early autumn in his boats and up the coast, but the southern point of Kamchatka had never been explored or mapped. It was thought to extend much farther south than it actually did. He could have explored it while he waited for winter in Bolsheretsk. When questioned about this later in Moscow, by Apraxin, he said that he had not been inclined at the time to trust the men and materials, which had been brought so far, and at such great cost in labor and suffering, in ships knocked together while he was not there to supervise their construction, in unknown seas. His argument was not a very good one, for these were the same ships that he had trusted to transport the same men and materials 650 miles across the cold, foggy Sea of Okhotsk, out of the sight of land all the way.

So they set out, and the Kamchadals—a race who had been defeated, murdered en masse when they tried to revolt, and kicked about until they had lost their vitality and most of their will to survive—took the brunt of it. They were answerable to Spanberg, who came between them and Bering, and Spanberg, remembering all too well what other natives had done to him on the Aldan and the Yudoma, made them pay for it. They were so knocked about by the work and the hardships imposed upon them that not many of them survived the trip, which took all winter. The treatment they received was a scandal for years in East Siberia, which was difficult to scandalize to any lasting extent, there being so much in the way of lies and scandal continually being hatched there.

It is probably unfair to put too much of the blame for this on Spanberg; the entire Expedition has to share it. He was a hard case, but so were they all by that time; they had been pushed too far for too long, and it had not gentled them any. It was far easier for them to overwork and beat up demoralized natives than it was to bestir their own weary bones, and even easier to starve them; who wanted to waste food that one had broken his back to move over hundreds of miles on an inferior race? These were people who threw their dead into the woods for the dogs to devour and put sick people out in the forest with food for a week, to recover or die by themselves. Even Bering got to the point of calling them a people who were strangers to all good customs, holders to evil practices who had no gods whatever. They would have had even a worse time of it if they hadn't been lucky enough to find a dead whale on the shore in the fall, from which they prepared several tons of blubbery provender to carry them through the trip.

The winter went on; the Expedition crawled forward between the ridges. Every evening they had to dig holes in the snow and cover them with canvas to sleep. It is difficult in these days of soft living to imagine the constant, wearing hardships and the iron difficulties of getting anchors, clumsy ships' tackle, tons of flour and whatnot through the *poorgas* of the Kamchatkan winter with temperatures occasionally hovering around fifty degrees below zero, after having already dragged most of it for thousands of freezing miles across Siberia. But they did it; they finally passed the perfect snow-covered cone of Klyuchevskaya, swung around the foothills of the mountains and reached the Lower Kamchatka Post on March 11. The Kamchadals who had managed to survive were paid off in Chinese tobacco and sent home.

chapter four

THE LOWER KAMCHATKA Post was a place of forty or fifty miserable shacks, a church, a palisaded fort and a monastery built half a mile away from the rest of the town. It was twenty miles from the sea, the farthest east of all the remote outposts of the empire, and was occupied by tribute collectors and Cossacks all grown as barbarous as the people they controlled. Sled dogs were the only domestic animals; they were so strong and good that they were sold on the mainland, but they were also so fierce and broke loose so often that any other animals the people tried to raise were killed by them; children sometimes fell victims to their ferocity. Spanberg was fascinated by these vicious beasts and presently got one for himself, beat it into obedience and thereafter set it upon anyone who displeased him.

The soil of Kamchatka was good, but there was so much dampness and so little sun, due to the fogs that were continually rolling in from the sea, that nothing much could be grown except root crops such as turnips; but the Kamchadals spent little time cultivating anything. They were a small people with brownish skins, broad, flat faces and black hair and eyes, honest and loyal to their friends; but the men were extremely lazy. They loved to drink brandy and talk endlessly together; they saw no virtue whatever in working any harder than they had to.

While the great spawning runs of salmon and other fish occurred in the rivers in the spring, they would bestir themselves for a while, net huge quantities of them, turn them over to the women to dry and relax again. The women also collected great quantities of berries and dug the root of a lily to pound into flour, which they used to thicken soup; in contrast to their men, they were always busy.

They all wore dogskin clothing, a suit of which lasted them for two or three years, and lived in underground houses that were made by roofing over a hole dug in the ground to a depth of eight feet or so, with a fifty-foot circumference. In their relaxed way they made out pretty well, what with the fish they caught, the berries and lily bulbs collected by their wives and the great number of birds' eggs they collected in the spring and put down in melted fish fat. The tax annually laid on each man of a seal, sea-otter, fox or sable skin or two was easily paid, and after catching the animal that supplied it, the men gave up hunting until the tax fell due again. The Russians, like the natives, ate fish—mostly raw—what roots they could dig, berries, ducks when they could catch them and the few whales that washed ashore and the seals that came their way. Occasionally they hunted bears, which they ate if they were lucky enough to kill them without getting killed themselves. They spent a great deal of time distilling their brandy, like the natives, from the sweet blue berries of the Kamchatkan honeysuckle and a grass known as "bear's foot." The March temperatures ranged around twenty degrees; the east coast was the warmest part of Kamchatka.

Bering found that the ship timbers had all been cut, trimmed by the carpenters Spanberg had taken from Okhotsk on his first trip and hauled to the river by dog teams. There was still plenty of snow; it would be with them until June. The carpenters began to build the ship on April 4, and the rest of the crew set to work to make caulking pitch from larch trees, distill liquor to take on the voyage and boil more sea water for salt. They caught a store of fish, which had started up the icy river to spawn, made butter from their oil and salted a great many of them.

The ship, which measured sixty feet by twenty, with a seven-and-a-half-foot draft, was finished during the first week of July. She was a two-master, brig-rigged. She was launched and christened St. Gabriel in one of the summer fogs that sometimes held for a week or more on that coast, and loaded with a store of provisions that would have caused even an amateur of nutrition some misgivings: salt beef, salt reindeer and salt fish. There was enough to last forty men for a year, if it did not kill them with scurvy first. There were forty-four of them, including a bailiff, two Cossacks, nine soldiers, six servants, a drummer and two Koryak interpreters. The Koryaks were from the north of Kamchatka, and more familiar with the Chukchi language than the Kamchadals from the south.

On the fourteenth they sailed out of the mouth of the Kamchatka River and into the Pacific. The voyage had begun; Bering had a deck under his feet again, after two and a half years and 6000 miles or so of the most desolate and difficult country on this earth, and now the unknown sea where he hoped to make his reputation a solid and enduring one stretched in front of him. He was forty-seven years old, not so resilient any more, a little more deliberate than he had ever been and still stout, heavy in body, despite the ground he had covered and the privations be-

65

hind him. He was still zealous to do his duty and a bit more; small details show it. Before sailing he had taken over to the monastery some rye and barley and had it sown because so little grain was grown there. Nobody bothered to tell him that it wouldn't grow to maturity.

After leaving the mouth of the river, they stood to the south to clear Point Africa, and later came about to follow the coast to the north in accordance with the Czar's instructions. On the sixteenth they were north of the Point. The coast range ended near the river, but the main range, inland behind the low coast, would be visible to them for several hundred miles—high, rugged and covered with snow on the summits even in summer. The country looked very bleak from the sea, and no one expected it to grow more hospitable as they advanced. They made a fair run for the day, but the wind dropped toward evening and the smoke of the cooking fires hung listlessly about the ship.

The next day, the seventeenth, fog moved in on them; they made little distance, and the rigging dripped dismally onto the deck. The next twenty-four hours were about the same, with scattered fogs and little breeze. On the twentieth and the twenty-first they had a favorable wind and logged 192 miles, added another hundred on the twenty-second, and did fairly well on the twenty-third. The coast grew higher and they held close to it to give the surveyors every opportunity to outline it on the maps they were making.

The twenty-fourth was a warm and pleasant day, so windless that the ship made little way but drifted in toward shore; most of them lay about on the deck for hours to sun the dank chill of the fog and the memory of the winter out of their bones. Little

66

progress was made on the twenty-fifth and not much more on the twenty-sixth. The fog came down again; it was too murky, even at night, for astronomical observations, and they didn't quite know where they were. On the twenty-seventh, however, they sighted Cape Thaddeus, which located them again, and doubled it at a distance of three miles.

They got around the Cape, but rain and fog came down on them on the twenty-eighth and forced them out to sea. There were many spotted whales, seals and dolphins about, appearing like ghosts and vanishing as silently into the mist. When the weather cleared sufficiently again they returned to within a mile of shore and anchored, and saw that the land had flattened out. They had left the mountains, the Koryak Range that had been with them for 300 miles, and were off the great low area of tundra that surrounds the basin of the Anadyr, the northernmost big river of eastern Asia which flows into the Pacific and which Deshneff had discovered nearly 100 years before. A boat was put over and the sub-lieutenant, Chaplin, took a detail ashore to look for fresh water and a good anchorage. He could see nothing in the way of a protected spot where the ship would hold in a blow, and there was no good running water on the tundra when he got ashore; he returned to the ship and she got under way again.

Between the thirtieth and the thirty-first they entered the Gulf of Anadyr, into which the Anadyr River empties; and because the last Russian post on the eastern coast was on the river and the country immediately around it was fairly well known, they sailed across the gulf without investigating the southern end of it. On the thirty-first they logged eighty-five miles and, toward evening, saw land extending along the northern horizon topped by snowy mountain peaks, dim and unsubstantial in the distance.

This was the Anadyr Range, the watershed divide between the rivers flowing into the Arctic Ocean and the Anadyr; over a mile high, with deep and rugged valleys carved by glaciers, the range was the last one between them and the Arctic Ocean, but they didn't know that. Well above the mouth of the Anadyr now, they were in unknown country where the rare visitors—Cossacks and tribute collectors—from Kamchatka or the lonely post on the Kolyma River didn't go. They were on the edge of Chukchi land, where lived the redoubtable people who could still outfight the Cossacks, and the watch and the lookouts were instructed to keep a sharp eye out. There had been an increasing amount of talk as they had moved north about the Chukchi, and now that they were on the edge of Chukchi country, there was more of it. The speculation in the fo'c'sle as to what would happen when they did find the wild men was a little nervous, for there had been a good deal of talk in Yakutsk and Okhotsk; and young Shestakov, who had joined them at Yakutsk, did not play down these people. He had been impressed by them. Being a Cossack himself, and having the Cossack's tough and profane scorn of most natives who could be pushed around, he had been sharply fetched up by a native who not only refused to be pushed but had contrived in his turn to push a number of Shestakov's brother Cossacks beyond the boundary of life and stood ready to push more of them.

The first of August dawned gloomily with fog and windy rain, and Bering moved out to get sea room; the day was spent beating cautiously back and forth to maintain position, over a leaden, foggy sea. The weather cleared that night, and morning found them sixteen miles off the coast. They moved in again, and in their maneuvering they found a great arm of the sea running inland which Bering named Holy Cross Bay. It was a bleakly beautiful place, surrounded by tundra, with misty mountains rising to the north, and Chaplin was sent ashore again for fresh water and to find anchorage. Once again he found neither, although two days were spent in the search.[1]

They stood out again; the mountains, snowy and grim, were closer to the shore now, and they sailed along the rocky coast until the sixth, when the lookout sighted another likely looking bay toward evening. The next morning Chaplin was sent ashore for the third time, and returned finally with twenty-two barrels of drinkable water. There was some excitement evident in him before he climbed aboard and when he did get on deck, after the barrels were hoisted up, he could hardly wait to report that he had found a hut, of great bones covered with skins, which had been recently lived in, and foot paths all about.

They moved on again, knowing now that they were close to the warlike people. The watches needed no more warning. A feeling of suspense settled over the ship and the falconets were loaded; and early in the morning on the eighth when the lookout sang out that there was a small boat approaching them from shore, everyone scrambled up on deck and lined the rail. Slow matches were lighted, and the men holding them moved to the guns. The soldiers loaded their muskets. The boat came on. It seemed to be made of driftwood, with skins stretched over it; it held eight bronzed, sturdy men clad in loose-fitting furs. There was a stolid and purposeful air about these people from a barren, cold and foggy land; they weren't gay or cheerful like the Tunguses of the Okhotsk coast. When they were close enough the Koryak inter-

[1] Berkh's map of 1823, taken from Chaplin's log, doesn't show this two-day stop, although Chaplin states that it was made.

preters began to scream at them, and they shouted back. The Koryaks said that they claimed to be Chukchi; they wanted to know where the white men came from, and what they wanted.

The ship's company lining the rail stared at the eight men from the unknown land who had such a redoubtable reputation, and the men stared curiously back at them; and although they had probably never seen a ship before, they did not seem unduly impressed by it. Bering, after a short conference with his officers, told the Koryaks to invite the savages aboard.

The crew drew together a little at this; the outlandish words flew back and forth and at first neither the Koryaks nor the savages seemed to comprehend each other very well. Presently, however, there appeared to be understanding. The eight men gestured and argued among themselves, and then one of them picked up several inflated seal bladders from the bottom of the boat, arranged them around himself and, with no apparent unease, got into the icy water and swam calmly to the ship.

He climbed aboard and stood dripping streams of frigid water to the deck, a bronze-skinned, black-haired, chunky man, looking curiously about and unconcerned with his soggy furs or the gaping white men who could quickly have done away with him. There was a vital air about him, missing in the Kamchadals, who had been beaten in bloody wars with the Cossacks, murdered in wholesale numbers, swindled and decimated by white men's diseases until they had lost their zest for life. This man came of a stubborn, intractable race, of people who ate their own lice, washed in urine, and were lewd, obscene, ribald and enduring; their language had no words for abstract ideas. Death was not a natural process to them. People didn't die but were killed by *kelet,* invisible malignant spirits who killed them by invisible means and frequently ate them, being particularly fond of their livers. They sacrificed dogs and deer to these spirits and were more or less protected from them by a deity called Big Raven, a companion and helper of the Creator. Big Raven had a wife called Miti, and the pair of them were full of indecent tricks with which they amused themselves; they turned their genitalia into dogs and people, laughed at their actions and changed them back again. Miti made puddings out of her vulva and fed Big Raven upon them; and Big Raven, when he traveled, believed in going unburdened. When he grew hungry he cut off his penis, turned it into a bird, which he sent off to bring back meat, and turned it back into the original article when it returned with food. When Big Raven and Miti began to grow old, they changed their sexual organs into talking dogs, which ran errands for them—something new in geriatrics.

Presently the boat moved closer, and the companions of the ship's visitor sat watching while Bering began asking his questions through the Koryaks. The Chukchi lived all along these shores, the savage answered, and they had heard of the Russians. Some of the Chukchi who kept deer had driven in their sleds overland to the Russian post on the Kolyma, which emptied into the sea which always had ice in it, and seen the Russians there. The ship, if it kept on, would soon come to an island in the sea where other Chukchi lived. Bering wanted to know if there were other islands or a large land ahead of him. The savage shook his head; he knew of neither. Bering sent Chaplin below for some small presents, which were given to their visitor. He tucked them under his jacket with no change of expression; then he went over the side, swam back to his boat and was pulled aboard by the others. He showed them his presents and by his gestures urged them to visit the ship;

but they decided to stay where they were, and nothing came of it. Presently they picked up their paddles, turned their boat about and set off for the bleak shore. The loom of the land swallowed them and they were gone. All that remained to remind the crew that they had had a visit from one of the people of that misty, bleak land of mountains and snow who had casually taken a swim in water cold enough to kill any of them in a few minutes was a little pool of that same water on the deck.

St. Gabriel went on her way; the nights were lighted by the midnight sun, during the few hours that the fog lifted enough for them to see it. For two days the winds were light, and they made little progress. The tenth saw them off the point of land where the coast turns to the north; they intended to follow it, but the fog came down on them so thickly that they lost their way. The compass was little good to them in those latitudes, and despite the fact that the current set toward the north, they somehow made a southeastern leg of fifty miles or so and came to an island that Bering named St. Lawrence.*

It burst upon them suddenly on the afternoon of the eleventh, when the fog cleared for a little. It was a bleak place; the hills, curiously refracted and taking on all the strange shapes caused by this phenomenon, rose one after another to a height of 500 feet or so, covered with snow on their tops. There were great numbers of seals and whales in the water, and birds flying all about. The island was so low in the center that the sea seemed to divide it. What with the refraction and the snow, the tatters of cold fog and the bold, sheer cliffs to the south, the place had an air at once

---

* The record here is very unclear. Berkh's map, based on Chaplin's log, does not show the ship's track anywhere near St. Lawrence, but Bering says in his report that they were there.

desolate, grim and other-worldly. Far off they could see the loom of the Asiatic shore, which located them, before the fog thickened again.

The lower parts of the island, below the snow line, were tree-less, bare of shrubs but green, and had a mossy look. Chaplin was sent ashore with a boat's crew, and although he found several na-tive dwellings half buried in the earth and roofed with driftwood poles and moss, he did not see any people. It was silent, except for bird cries, and eerie; he was afraid the fog would catch him, and didn't stay very long.

When he was back on board, *St. Gabriel* was headed for the Siberian shore again and stayed close to it on a northerly course the rest of the night and the next day, when there was little wind and scant progress made. The wind freshened and they made ninety-four miles on the thirteenth, putting them above East Cape, which looked like an island from the sea. They were aslo past the Diomedes, which they didn't see in the fog, although they had been very close to them.

On the afternoon of the thirteenth they calculated that their position was 65° 30' north; the land, as far as they could see, faded into the west. There was no visible loom of land in all their view to the north, no indication that the Asiatic continent turned to-ward the direction where America should be.

Bering called for a conference with his officers to determine what should be done. August was half over, he said, and they well knew what that meant; an early autumn had caught Spanberg between Yakutsk and Okhotsk, much farther south than they were now, and in their present latitude, winter would be earlier and more severe. No one knew how severe it would be, but it was sure to be very bad. Should they go farther north, and if so, how

73

far? According to the Chukchi who had come aboard the ship, they were past the easternmost point of Asia, and nothing lay beyond it. Should they begin to look for harbors, should they plan on spending the dark winter somewhere along this coast? Where did it seem best, from the standpoint of best serving Russia, to go for the winter to protect the ship and the crew from conditions of which they really knew nothing?

There was a silence and then Spanberg, being the senior lieutenant, gave his opinion. They were very far north, he said, and the bleak Chukchi coast, stretching away from them and far to the south, was without usable harbors or any wood to burn. How would they protect the ship or keep themselves warm when the winter weather of that latitude finally came down on them with its bitter cold and darkness? Besides that, the Chukchi were not a peaceful people, as they all knew. It was true that several of these savages had come out to look at them and behaved themselves, but young Shestakov—who had fought them with his uncle—had told them that it took very little to turn a seemingly peaceful Chukchi into a wildly raging one. Spanberg was far from a fearful man, but he said candidly that he didn't like the look of the place nor could he see any profit in staying there for the winter. The ice might seize them or crush the ship, and then how would they return? No, he said, he did not think their chances of survival here were good. He thought they should continue to sail north until the sixteenth, and if they hadn't reached sixty-six degrees north by then, they should return to Kamchatka for the winter.

Chirikov, who had been looking at the deck, shook his head and looked up. They both wanted to return to Kamchatka and he could understand that, he said; but he begged leave to differ with them. No one knew, he said, how far any man had been to the north in the Arctic Ocean above Siberia; consequently, they couldn't be sure that Siberia and America weren't joined somewhere west of East Cape unless they sailed around to the mouth of the Kolyma, or as far in that direction as the ice, if they encountered it, would let them go. They knew there was no joining of the continents west of the Kolyma; but they would have to go to the Kolyma to prove there was no joining east of it. Peter's orders, he went on, had been to touch at a place under European jurisdiction; if there was no such place to the west of them, they would prove it by going to the Russian post on the Kolyma. If the land they saw to the west finally turned north somewhere beyond their present view and they couldn't reach the Kolyma, then they should look for winter quarters by the twenty-fifth of the month . . . probably somewhere opposite East Cape where, he had heard from young Shestakov, who had heard it from the Chukchi, there was a forested land.

This was a remarkably logical and courageous opinion from a junior officer who had usually been relegated to the rear. It gave Bering and Spanberg something to think about, and there was a long silence. It was not broken by Spanberg; he had given his opinion, and wasn't the man to change it. Bering took a turn around the deck, obviously uncomfortable, for Chirikov had brought out several things that disturbed him. Peter's orders, for one thing; and a feeling, undefined because his mind kept it in the background, that Chirikov was a better man for the job than either Spanberg or himself because he had the true explorer's spirit and was willing to dare more.

He could have said to himself that Chirikov was a crazy Russian and not altogether responsible, and perhaps he did; it was his only defense against a feeling of inadequacy that he could not admit to himself. He looked off to the west again and, in all that desolate sweep of sea and sky, failed once more to see land stretching to the north; he thought of adverse winds that might come up and hold him above East Cape until the ice got him and he couldn't return; he knew that he didn't want to face winter in those latitudes and the Chukchi. If he wavered he got no support in his wavering from Spanberg. Finally, to his future sorrow, he rejected Chirikov's advice and sided with the senior lieutenant. They would go north a little farther, he said, and then return; nothing more was mentioned about Chirikov's suggestion, based only upon some Chukchi gossip that Chirikov had heard somewhere, that they investigate farther to the east.

Bering's decision, which confirmed in a way Apraxin's opinion that he wasn't active enough in body or spirit, was in character. He was a sailor, bred in the tradition of taking his ship and crew somewhere and bringing them back in safety. Apraxin had been trying to say that there was not enough fire in him, that he was too careful, or too torpid, to be an explorer, and that was possibly true. Peter, who knew him as an expert in transportation, had been thinking of the trip to Kamchatka; Apraxin had been thinking of what was to be done after Kamchatka was reached.

If Spanberg, that hard man, had given him—or Chirikov—a bit more encouragement, Apraxin might have been proved wrong; or if Bering had been a bit more daring, his luck might have been better. For luck often has a way of favoring a daring man.

They went on, meeting occasional drift ice, until three o'clock in the afternoon of the fifteenth, when they reached 67° 18′ north latitude. There was still no sight of land anywhere; even the Asiatic coast was now too far to the south and the west to see.

Bering gave the order to come about and set the course for Kamchatka. There was a feeling of relief throughout the ship except for Chirikov, and he refrained from any further comment.

The wind was at their backs now, and they made good progress for the rest of the day and the night. The next morning was foggy, and presently another island suddenly loomed up to the port. It was, like St. Lawrence, rocky and bleak. It had low rocky cliffs on the northwest end, and small rocky points off shore breaking the water. The other end of it faded off into the mist, and Bering decided not to circumnavigate it. He named it St. Diomede, and we call it Big Diomede today.

There are three islands in this group, of which Big Diomede is the most westerly one. If Bering had decided to investigate it, to sail around it, he might well have seen the second island and possibly the third one—and just as possibly the American shore. If he had stayed in the vicinity long enough for this, the fog might have cleared long enough to let him see America. When Cook sailed the strait later he was luckier, for the sun dispersed the fog long enough for him to see both continents. Bering Strait is only forty miles wide at this point; Big Diomede is less than twenty-five miles from the Siberian coast.

Bering had sailed between Big Diomede and Siberia both going north and coming south again. He hadn't seen the island on the northward trip, due to fog, and glimpsed it and gone on when he returned. It can be argued that he was very casual with his exploring as he headed for home, but he was certainly mishandled by fortune.

It is fruitless but rather interesting to speculate about what would have happened if Bering's luck with the weather had been as good as Cook's and he had seen the American shore. He was not the first man to be brought to grief by a bit of foggy North Pacific weather, but the margin was so narrow in his case that he was certainly among the unluckiest. It was most unfortunate for him that he did not sail about a bit more while he was in the north, and rather hard to understand. Perhaps it can be explained by the fact that he was a sailor, not an explorer, and probably the majority of sailors would have done the same thing under the circumstances. They are trained in their calling to go from one point to another and not linger on the way or indulge in fanciful side trips; and perhaps in a lifetime of following the sailors' trade, this became a habit of thought that Bering could not break or even think of breaking.

chapter
five

AFTER LEAVING Big Diomede, *St. Gabriel* sailed before a fair wind
and sighted St. Lawrence Island again, in the distance, on the
seventeenth. On the twentieth, not far from where they had seen
the Chukchi before, they were approached by four native skin
boats with about forty Chukchi in them. This was a considerable
increase in force over their former visitors, and there was some
uneasy speculation as to whether the presents given to the savage
who had boarded them had aroused ideas of rapine. Everything
that would shoot was hastily prepared for action, but the visitors
were inclined toward peace. They held up several walrus tusks
and fox skins, waving them about over their heads to show that
they wanted to trade. They were motioned to approach, and soon
swarmed on board.

They had a miscellaneous collection of objects with them: deer
meat, fish, fresh water, a few red and blue fox skins and four
walrus tusks. In their usual rather superior fashion they laid out
their property and left the bargaining to the Russians, scornfully
shaking their heads until an offer was made that interested them.
The crew ran about from one of them to the other, offering needles, knives and similar things. While this was going on, one of

79

the Koryaks took several of them to the officers. Bering questioned them again. One of the Chukchi volunteered the information that he knew the Russians; he had been to the fort on the Anadyr and seen them before. None of them had ever been to the Kolyma, but some of their friends had been there, riding overland on their deer. No one among them went to the Kolyma by sea and, indeed, didn't know whether it could be done; it was too difficult to sail around East Cape and get through the ice, too far and too much trouble. At this point the other Chukchi, having finished their trading, began getting back into their skin boats, and the ones who had been talking to Bering joined them.

St. Gabriel sailed on. They passed Transfiguration Bay that day and sighted St. Thaddeus Mountain a day later; then a four-day calm practically immobilized them until the twenty-fifth, when a fair breeze came up and took them almost to Point Africa. As they closed the shore on the thirtieth, already finished with the voyage in their minds, a sudden gust of wind out of nowhere, violent and freakish, struck them like a blow of a gigantic hammer. It ripped the mainsail and the foresail to tatters, made a cat's cradle of the rigging and drove them at the rocks.

For a short space they were all stunned by it. It was like a betrayal, an inexplicable savage stroke by a fortune that had carried them safely through the unknown foggy seas where they had never felt secure for a moment to drown them around the corner from home. They were shaken out of their confusion by the reeling of the ship and the roaring of the breakers on the rocks ashore, the pandemonium of those below fighting one another to get on deck, and the shouting of the officer on watch. They settled down just in time to get an anchor over to hold *St. Gabriel* off the rocks, and presently the wind fell as quickly as it had come up. As soon as the sea flattened out and the ship ceased her wild bucking, Spanberg had them swarming over her to repair the damage, for they were in a bad position if a storm should come up.

It took them all that night, by the light of torches, and all the next day to get back into sailing condition again. The day after that they set out, and the following day they reached the mouth of the Kamchatka River. Then the wind grew contrary again; it was five more days before they could sail up the river and go ashore.

Bering thought it too late in the year to cross the peninsula and sail for Okhotsk with the conditions that held in the Sea of Okhotsk in autumn, and so they prepared to spend the winter at Lower Post. It may have been, now that the voyage was over and so little concrete had come of it, that Bering was plagued by shadowy second thoughts and felt reluctant to go home at once and report upon what he had done. He had not, since early in the trip, delayed because of winter weather, and on the return trip he would be traveling light. Possibly, as the days shortened and there was less to do, he fell to reviewing what had been done and recalled Chirikov's opinion at their most northerly point: that they should go to the Russian post on the Kolyma, as Peter had ordered, or sail farther to the east, where there may have been a new and forested land. He must have realized that he hadn't fully followed his orders, and secretly have been dismayed that he had so quickly come out of the north. These are the sort of thoughts that are liable to come upon a man during long and empty evenings after the responsibilities of shipboard no longer preoccupy him.

After they were all settled down, he began to hunt up as many of the old residents of Kamchatka as were nearby and to talk to them. He finally found several who believed that there was land

81

to the east of the peninsula, for they remembered that there had been a man, back in 1715, who was not a native of Kamchatka and who had claimed that he had been captured while hunting on Karaginski Island, off the coast to the northward, and brought to Lower Post. This man, according to their recollections, had said that he was from somewhere east of Kamchatka; there were forests in the land he had come from, and rivers that ran into the Kamchatka Sea, and his people used skin boats, like the Kamchadals.

These conversations, unlike the rumors and tales that Bering had heard in Yakutsk, that gathering place of traders and wandering travelers in the north, were disturbing; they kept in the forefront of his mind all the shadowy possibilities of the land that he hadn't found. The rumors he had heard on the way out were vague enough but exciting, but these present rumors were in the nature of a reproach. He had never quite believed the first ones that there was a land to the north of the Kolyma, and he believed them less now that he had been in the northern sea and had a look for himself; further, the first Chukchi who had boarded them had said he had never heard of land to the north. By reports there was always ice in the northern sea above Siberia and the Kolyma was frozen most of the year. Who could sail north from the Kolyma and see this improbable land? The rumors were not based on anything. The Chukchi wouldn't do it; they wouldn't even try to sail around East Cape; and no skin boats that the Cossacks would build—not to mention the fact that Cossacks weren't sailors—could live in such a place.

So much for that; he convinced himself. But the possible land to the east which Chirikov had heard about was something else again. One could sail the sea in that direction; he had done it himself; and the captive the old people remembered, who certainly

82

would not have traveled very far merely to hunt, *could* have come over it from the east, from the elusive continent of America or even from the equally elusive Gamaland or Companyland, which all the geographers said were there.

These thoughts plagued him through the uncomfortable winter in the miserable surroundings of Lower Post among the even more miserable people who lived there, and as soon as anything could be done in the spring, he got the crew into action and put the ships into sailing condition again. On June 6, 1729, *Fortune* sailed for Bolsheretsk and *St. Gabriel* put out to sea. Bering set an east-by-south course and held it for two days before a light breeze, with the lookouts doubled. The wind picked up on the seventh and increased on the eighth. On the late afternoon of that day Bering gave up hope of seeing the land he longed for and came about on a south-by-southwest course. If he had only gone on for a few more hours he would have sighted the Commander Islands, where some years later he was to die in a cold hole in the sand. He seemed always to be fated to miss everything he looked for by the narrowest of margins.

The winds were variable on the ninth, and he changed course to the south. From then until the seventeenth, when he reached about the same latitude as the southern tip of Kamchatka, he wandered over quite a bit of sea. On the seventeenth, still having seen nothing, he headed north again, and on the twenty-second he was off Cape Kronotski.

He closed the coast and sailed down it, mapping it as he went, and saw the splendid harbor at Avacha Bay which was to be Petropavlovsk, the staging point of the Second Expedition, lying beneath the beautiful snowy cone of Avacha Volcano. Continuing on, he sailed around the southern tip of the peninsula and

83

made the Bolshaya River on July 2, a year and ten months after he had dropped anchor there on the trip out. The southern coast of Kamchatka had finally been mapped. The supplies that remained, about fourteen and a half tons of flour, dried meat, salt and groats, were sent ashore to be divided between Bolsheretsk and Lower Kamchatka posts.

Fortune had been waiting for Bering off the mouth of the Bolshaya, and the two ships sailed for Okhotsk, which they reached ten days later. The ships were turned over to the port authorities, and Bering and his crew started out for St. Petersburg. They traveled steadily over the same route that had brought them east; their only layover was at the village of Peleduye, and only long enough there for the ice on the Lena to get firm enough for travel. There were hardships, but at least they missed the hordes of bloodsucking insects that had made their lives a misery on the way out. They reached St. Petersburg on the last day of February 1730, filthy, fined down and tired to their bones. They had seen new seas and lands that no European had looked upon before; stony, unknown islands had appeared to them out of the North Pacific fogs, which ironically had given them a little and then hidden from them the land they had suffered so much to find. They had charted hundreds of miles of unknown coasts; but they hadn't found America or confirmed the geographers in their baseless fancies about lands that had never existed. Now that they were back, they would soon be told how utterly they had failed.

I would like to make a digression at this point to include a not altogether extraneous bit of history as a sort of footnote upon Bering's luck. In the beginning it has to do with the Cossack chief Afanase Shestakov, whose nephew had joined Bering at

Yakutsk and made the trip with him. The elder Shestakov had conceived a notion of an expedition to conquer the Chukchi and northern Koryaks in northeast Siberia and collect tribute from them, and in 1727 when Bering was in Okhotsk, he laid this notion before the Senate in St. Petersburg. The Senate approved his plans; he was given authority to bring the natives to heel and explore, and 1500 men were given him. Almost as an afterthought, however, the Senate decided not to give him complete command. He had to accept as co-commander a man named Dimitri Pavlutski, a captain of dragoons, who was appointed by the governor of Siberia. Shestakov was a difficult man to get along with at the best of times, and the division of authority galled him; he began to quarrel with Pavlutski, who gave as good as he got. Their squabbles got so acrimonious that the entire force grew badly demoralized. They wasted a month at Ilimsk before their differences could be temporarily patched up, and parted at Yakutsk; Pavlutski was left there to take the force to the Anadyr, and Shestakov went on to Okhotsk to get the ships Bering had left there and upon his return sail up the Kamchatkan coast to meet Pavlutski.

Bering had left for St. Petersburg by the time Shestakov got to Okhotsk, so he took over St. Gabriel and Fortune, and built two other ships. St. Gabriel was to explore the coast south of Okhotsk; Fortune was to chart the Kuriles; Shestakov took the other two ships himself, sailed around Kamchatka and headed for the Anadyr. The two ships became separated. Shestakov's ship was becalmed and fogged in partway up the coast, and, deciding to march the rest of the way and build several forts en route, he sent her back. On his march he fought several small engagements with the Chukchi and defeated them, but presently, living up to their reputation, they brought up a force to equal his own, killed him

85

and most of his men and dispersed the rest. The other ship was finally captured and burned by the Chukchi, and most of her people were killed. The people who had gone off in *St. Gabriel* and *Fortune* turned out to be so incompetent that that portion of Shestakov's enterprise also came to nothing, and the two ships returned to Okhotsk.

Pavlutski, for his part, managed matters differently; he was a good man. He left Yakutsk and went north to the post on the Kolyma, where he wintered. He heard of Shestakov's death the following April and ordered *St. Gabriel,* now back at Okhotsk, to sail for the Anadyr. *St. Gabriel* sailed so late that she had to winter at Bolsheretsk, and the following spring Pavlutski ordered her again to the Anadyr, having come overland from the Kolyma himself in the meantime and taken up his quarters at the Anadyr post. There was something new in her orders this time, however; instead of merely bringing men and material to Pavlutski, *St. Gabriel* was to touch at the Anadyr post and then go search for the American continent and collect tribute from the natives.

St. Gabriel left Bolsheretsk on April 22, 1732, under command of a man named Fedorof, who was so ill he had to be carried aboard. He never recovered sufficiently to take command, which devolved upon a surveyor named Micheal Gwosdef. Among Gwosdef's crew there was a sailor named Moshkof, who had sailed with Bering, and Moshkof told Gwosdef about Big Diomede. Gwosdef was so intrigued by this information that he didn't even stop at the Anadyr post. He reached Anadyrski Cape on August 2, went ashore for water, killed two deer and took off again. He sighted two Chukchi in skin boats the next day, but they would have nothing to do with him, and the day after he took nine men ashore to the place from which the two Chukchi had come. All he could find was two huts made of whalebone and covered with earth, and two men who ran away when they saw him.

They sailed about for several days more, and saw a few more Chukchi who refused to pay tribute when asked for it. A week or so later they sighted an island, but owing to a head wind they couldn't get near it; they had to lay-to close to East Cape, watched by many Chukchi on shore, until the wind shifted, and then sailed for the island, which was one of the Diomedes. They made an attempt to land; but the bush telegraph had apparently got the word about Shestakov's ambitions even to those remote parts and the islanders were taking no chances. They received Gwosdef's boats with a shower of arrows. The Russians returned this discourtesy with musket fire; but presently some basis for conversation must have been established, for Gwosdef says that after considerable difficulty they learned that the archers were Chukchi, and that some of their people had fought against Pavlutski around the Anadyr. It seemed obvious that no tribute would be forthcoming in that vicinity, so Gwosdef circumnavigated the island and tried unsuccessfully to collect tribute again on the other side of it.

He landed and examined several native houses, and from that spot saw another of the Diomedes, and, still further beyond it to the east, the third Diomede and the American continent.

They left the first island and sailed to the second one, where another flight of arrows discouraged them from landing. They went on, and anchored about four and a half miles off the continent, or the third island. Gwosdef isn't very clear about this; he apparently always thought that the American continent was an island, a fourth one, and in his report uses "island" and the "Large Country" (a name sometimes for the mysterious American continent) indiscriminately. He can hardly be blamed for it; he didn't know America was there, or what he was looking at; but it makes for confusing reading.

At any rate, they couldn't approach the third Diomede (or the American shore) because of head winds and shallow water, so they sailed on to the fourth island (or the American shore) and tried to get close to it. A strong wind came up and the sails gave way. The sailors, who were as confused as Gwosdef, decided that they had had enough of it at this manifestation; they came to Gwosdef and asked to be taken back to Kamchatka. There was an argument, and while it was going on, a native—an Eskimo or an Aleut—approached them in a kayak, the first they had seen. He was darker than the Chukchi, with more angular features, snug and waterproof in a shirt of whale intestines which fastened around the cockpit of the kayak. The interpreter aboard could understand him in a measure; he said that the Chukchi (a word doubtless used by the interpreter) lived in the place they saw, which had forests, streams and animals in it, and presently headed back to shore again.

Thus the Russians first saw a man from the New World, and thought he was a Chukchi. They wasted little time wondering about him. Gwosdef dismisses him in his report by saying that they could not get close enough to the shore to tell whether the native was telling the truth or not, and as soon as he turned away, the crew started their demands to be taken home again. The season was growing late, they said, God knew what powers of darkness informed the unknown land, and winter storms were due. A formal meeting was held and a petition was drawn up and signed by everybody; Gwosdef gave in. St. Gabriel was headed for Kamchatka, and reached the mouth of the Kamchatka River on Sep-

88

tember 28, 1732, two years and seven months after Bering got back to St. Petersburg.

A report of the voyage and the discovery was immediately sent in, and no one knows what became of it. Fedorof, the nominal commander during the voyage, died in February of the next year, and it was not until July that Gwosdef, wondering why no one in an official position had asked him about the trip, sent in the ship's logbook and a brief report to Okhotsk. They were also lost. The Admiralty College in St. Petersburg knew nothing whatever about the trip until 1738, when they were trying one of the sailors who had been sent to the capital from Tobolsk on a criminal charge, and the sailor spoke of the voyage.

The importance of the voyage was immediately realized and inquiries were made; but the bureaucracy of East Siberia had other fish to fry, as usual, and not even an Imperial order in 1742 stirred them up. Spanberg, who had succeeded Bering in command in the east, then took hold of things. He hunted Gwosdef up, got another report from him in 1743, and sent it to the Admiralty College. It had been eleven years since Gwosdef had seen the "Large Country" and sent in his first report, and by the time the Admiralty received the details, Bering had been dead for almost two years.

Had he known of Gwosdef's discovery, it might have made no difference whatever; he might have been thrown completely off by Gwosdef's confusion of "Large Countries" and islands, but one is inclined to think otherwise. Had he read the report or been able to talk to Gwosdef, it might have given him a direction to move in, a knowledge of the distance he had to cope with and a firm idea of the time at his disposal for the Second Expedition to go to America and return safely. Instead, the report was used to start a fire or thrust into a pigeonhole in a desk in Okhotsk, Yakutsk or Tobolsk and forgotten.

Bering handed in his report and went home to his wife, and for a few days there was silence. He thought little of it, being preoccupied by the business of getting accustomed to good food, a clean bed, the warmth and comfort of a house and all of the other delights of civilization again after the cold fogs of the North Pacific and the bleak and wintry emptiness of Siberia. It was strange and difficult to get used to being warm and clean once more, to be freed of the constant responsibility of keeping life and direction in himself and his crew in sub-zero temperatures, of sleeping in a bed with a woman. At first he did little but eat and sleep, and then began to go about among his friends.

Those who liked him listened to the stories of his adventures and were warm in their admiration and congratulations, but just a little over his immediate horizon a fine storm was brewing. It started among the officers of the Admiralty and in the Senate, to which places his report had gone and received an unenthusiastic reception by the majority in both. They held that in the main Bering had done a good job in view of the tremendous difficulties he had encountered, but that he hadn't got what he had gone after.

There was a political upheaval in the making, and official St. Petersburg was on edge to begin with. After Catherine had died in 1727 and Peter's twelve-year-old grandson had been made Czar, power had passed to the Supreme Privy Council, which was composed of Peter's new nobility; but the Church and the old nobility had moved in and replaced most of them with the old reactionaries, who had been against the westernization, and anything that smacked of it was due for an uneasy time. The first intimation

Bering had of this was when the Admiralty called him in for questioning, and it was a rude awakening for him after the congratulations of his friends.

They weren't vindictive or harsh; they treated him civilly enough; but the imposing Admiralty rooms and the gathering of high officials was unnerving and they started in by asking him why he hadn't sailed around to the mouth of the Kolyma. So long as he had not explored the Arctic coast between the Kolyma and East Cape he could not assure them that there wasn't a land bridge to a large country in that area, and to do that exploring had been the reason why he had been sent.

Standing before them, shocked but forthright and serious, he repeated his report to the effect that he had been unable to see any land whatever from his northern point.

But why hadn't he gone farther? they asked. To sail to the Kolyma had been in his orders. Doubtless he had heard the Siberian rumors that there was a large land north of the Kolyma, and another to the east of East Cape? Had he proved that these were rumors or fact? He had inquired of the Chukchi he had encountered, he said, and they knew nothing of these rumored lands. At this, someone remarked that he had not been sent all that distance to collect the suppositions of the Chukchi.

Why, they repeated, hadn't he sailed around East Cape to the west? They brought out some of his correspondence, sent back from Yeniseisk in 1725; for a time he had tried to get his orders changed so that he could go to the Kolyma instead of Okhotsk, build a ship there, and sail east around East Cape. If he had wanted to sail east from the Kolyma, why hadn't he wanted to sail west to reach it? He couldn't answer them.

Earnestly, even a little desperately now, he tried to persuade them that he had done his duty. They couldn't realize the difficulties, he said. As far north as he dared go, blinded by cold and impenetrable fogs most of the time, he had to consider the safety of his ship and his crew.

But why had he sailed north instead of west, along the Arctic coast? Why, so far as that went, hadn't he gone farther to the east, where Siberian rumor had it there was a large country?

He couldn't reply. He thought of Chirikov's advice at sixty-six degrees north latitude, and was silent. They were all looking at him; the silence stretched out; finally he quoted the end of his report, justifying his return. If he had gone farther and met with head winds, he said, it would have been impossible to return that summer. To winter in those regions was out of the question, because there were no forests and the people were not under Russian jurisdiction but did as they pleased.

They saw that he had no more to offer them, and ended the interview. He would hear from them, they said, and thanked him for coming. There was no irony in their thanks; they still thought him a man of ability who had somehow got off the track. They were kind enough, but there was no doubt whatever that they thought he had failed. He went home like a man with an immense weight bowing his back.

chapter six

WHAT HAPPENED TO Bering was bad enough, but there was worse to come. The Academy of Sciences, which was to suffer eclipse later, had not been much disturbed after Catherine's death when the conservatives of the old nobility came back into power and moved the seat of government back to Moscow; the old nobility were soon turned out when the Empress Anna took the throne, and there hadn't been time for them to interfere with the Academy. The Academicians were still intolerant, quarrelsome and superior, and, like many other scientific men of that period and others, bigoted and extremely scornful of any opinion except their own. There were a number of prejudices, misconceptions and outright inventions among them. Guillaume Delisle, the foremost geographer of his day while he lived, had invented or been the foremost supporter of the two mythical lands Gamaland and Companyland, which he said came close to Yezo, which was close to Kamchatka; when Bering returned with charts, having sailed around Kamchatka as well as taken an additional trip toward the east and wandered over a fair amount of ocean without finding any of these lands, Guillaume's surviving brother, Nicolas, felt that he had to uphold the family honor and refute him. Another

93

Academy member, Gerhard Müller, who had never been beyond the Urals, was vociferous on all occasions in declaring that Bering had obviously never reached the eastern point of Asia. Shestakov, before his death at the capable hands of the Chukchi, had drawn up a number of crude and incorrect sketch maps of northeastern Siberia out of his head, for he had never been to East Cape and hadn't the vaguest idea of the geography thereabouts; but Delisle accepted these maps and would have no part of Bering's.

The scientific gentry drew together and clung to the inventions of Guillaume Delisle and the cartographers, which had been spread all over the world by their charts and maps, and they were most vocal and contentious doing it. They couldn't admit that they had been proved wrong by an ignorant sailor who hadn't even carried out his orders. They swung in behind Delisle and Müller, and froze Bering out. When his map was made in Moscow in 1731, they had enough influence in the government to have it discredited; the government gave it to the King of Poland, who finally gave it to the Jesuit Du Halde. The otherwise influential Ivan Kiriloff, who published his general map of Russia in 1734, wanted to accept Bering's map but could get no one in the Academy to agree with him that it was usable; and three years later, when the Academy published its map of Asia, there was no discernible evidence of Bering's discoveries on it.

It can be seen from all this that the Academicians hated Bering virulently, with a hatred that was to last for years; they did their best to discredit him after he returned. For a while he had a very thin time. He hid his diminished head and brooded; he thought of the endless days and nights in the freezing cold of Siberia and the bone-chilling fogs of the North Pacific, of the empty, unknown, inimical ocean at his northern point, of the stupid, superior stubbornness of the geographers who never left St. Petersburg and crammed their baseless Gamalands down his throat. It was this kind of thing, in its unfairness, that galled him and filled him with bitterness. He had always tried to be a reasonable man; he realized now that he should have followed Chirikov's advice and sailed to the west, and that the criticism that fell upon him for not doing it was more or less just. That his discoveries and maps, which were concrete things, should be sneered at and denied out of sheer caprice or malice was something else again.

It was a thing that a man had to accept, however; he couldn't change it. The Academicians were riding high and he couldn't combat them. As he came to accept the conditions in which he found himself, during the sleepless nights, he arrived at a determination to try to be sent out again. He wanted to vindicate himself, and so he went to work on a proposal to be sent to the Empress Anna Ivanovna, one of Peter's nieces from Courland on the Baltic, who had been invited to the throne by the Supreme Privy Council after Peter II died in 1730. The Council had made her sign a set of limiting conditions which would reserve a great deal of power for them; but she got the Guards officers on her side by promising them that under her rule the length of their service in the army (which Peter had never limited) would be shortened; then the Council gave her their support. She ascended the throne, the conditions were torn up, the Council was dissolved, and the autocracy was back again. The influence of foreigners was much strengthened again at court.

Finally Bering had his proposition finished:

1- According to my observation, the waves of eastern Kamchatka are smaller than in other seas, and I found on Karaginski Island large fir trees that do not grow on Kamchatka. These signs indicate that America, or some other land on this side of it is not far from Kamchatka—perhaps from 150 to 200 miles. This could easily be ascertained by building a vessel of about 50 tons and sending it to investigate. If this be so (the existence of such a country), a trade might be established between the Empire and the inhabitants of those regions.

2- Such a ship should be built in Kamchatka, because the necessary timber could be obtained more easily. The same holds true in the matter of food—fish and game are especially cheap there. Then, again, more help may be obtained from the natives of Kamchatka than from those of Okhotsk. One other reason should not be overlooked: the mouth of the Kamchatka River is deeper and offers a better shelter for boats.

3- It would not be without advantage to find a sea route from the Kamchatka or Okhota River to the Amus River or Japan, since it is known that these regions are inhabited. It would be very profitable to open trade relations with these people, particularly the Japanese. And as we have no ships there (in the Okhotsk Sea), we might arrange it with the Japanese that they meet us halfway in their boats. For such an expedition a ship about the size of the one mentioned would be needed, or one somewhat smaller might serve the purpose.

4- The cost of such an expedition—not including salaries, provisions and materials for both boats, which cannot be had there and would have to be taken from here and Siberia—would be from 10,000 to 12,000 rubles.

5- If it should be considered wise to map the northern regions of the coast of Siberia—from the Ob to the Yenisei and from there to the Lena—this could be done by boats or by land, since these regions are under Russian jurisdiction.

This proposal was received with considerable interest, because it embodied and brought together a number of different ideas which had been put forward by a number of different people. Not long after Bering returned from the First Expedition in 1730, there began to be talk about another Expedition, and by 1731 arrangements were under way for it. These arrangements were confused because everyone wanted something different; some thought primarily of territorial expansion or new naval bases, some thought of foreign trade, some wanted new lands in which to explore for precious metals, and the Empress, along with the liberals who had come into power with her, wanted to impress Europe with Russia's progress in science and exploration.

There was also the question as to how the Expedition should be sent out. Count Golovin and Admiral Sanders each submitted memos to Anna suggesting that all transportation to Kamchatka be by sea, that ships be chartered to send everything necessary around Cape Horn to Kamchatka by way of Japan instead of trying to transport it by land across Siberia, the Sea of Okhotsk, and across Kamchatka. After resting the crews and refitting in Kamchatka, the ships were to be sent out again to explore the North Pacific. There was a good deal to be said for this idea, because it took into consideration the sufferings of the natives during the First Expedition, but it was finally turned down. By this time it had been decided to send scientists from the Academy to study the people, resources and other pertinent matters about Siberia and the new countries to be discovered, survey the Arctic coast from the White Sea all the way to Kamchatka, and chart the Kurile Islands and the way to Japan. It was thought that a land-based leader of these various enterprises could keep in

97

closer touch with all of them than a leader circumnavigating the world.

Bering was finally decided upon as commander because it was thought that he had done pretty well—although not as well as everyone had hoped—on the First Expedition; that his partial failure had been a salutary lesson to him; and that with this lesson and his experience he was the best man for the job. He was, of course, much pleased. He had got his second chance. He moved from conference to conference and worked late into the nights on the problems of the organization of the Expedition, which was daily growing more unwieldy and complicated. If he realized this, he didn't realize it clearly enough to protest; he was too busy, and in any event he had got himself into it. The innumerable details, the excitement and bustle of setting out again, and the satisfaction he felt at getting another chance—as Captain Commander of such an important enterprise—to exonerate himself all helped to blind him to the fact that possibly he—or any other man, for that matter—would find it too much to cope with. As the plans matured and the things that the Expedition were to do multiplied, it became evident to a number of other people that this was to be no simple exploration but the most ambitious and far-reaching one ever attempted.

By 1732 the Admiralty had made up its mind about what it wanted the Expedition to accomplish, and the official order, naming Bering as Captain Commander and Chirikov and Spanberg as Captains of the third class under him, was announced by the Senate on April 17; this was followed on May 2 by a general outline of what was to be done. All northern Asia was to be mapped, and the Siberian coast of the Arctic Ocean as well as the American coast as far south as California; two ships were to be built in Kamchatka to search for America, three more to survey the Kurile Islands, Japan, and the remaining areas of eastern Siberia, and several others—which were to be built in Siberia—to go up the Ob and the Lena to the Arctic coast and map the rivers and the coast. To take care of all this construction and the consequent activities of this three-pronged affair, Bering would have to get together, transport, oversee and feed for years a small army of people thousands of miles from home in a practically trackless wilderness that just about managed to support the few barbaric tribes who lived in it.

Besides this, he was ordered to establish navigational schools and iron mines and construct lighthouses, shipyards, foundries, rope walks, depots, villages to house his people while the ships were under construction and whatnot.

Nor was this all. The Academy of Sciences had been busily elaborating plans of its own and, before it was through, had decided to investigate the biology, ethnology, anthropology, linguistics and history of all Siberia and the lands to be discovered. This, of course, entailed some of the learned professors and their retinue of aides, secretaries, interpreters, artists, servants and even families in some cases; libraries, instruments and whatnot for nine or ten years. All these people had to be transported, housed and fed in a manner suitable to their dignity; they were to be independent of the naval command and not under its orders, although the navy had to provide for them.

All this would seem to need the powers of a dictator to hold together, but Bering wasn't given such powers. Although the civil authorities of Siberia were ordered to aid him as much as possible, he had to consult with them on an equal basis; he had to poll his ships' crews and consult with the Academicians on all important decisions; and, finally, he was ordered to get the approval of his Russian assistant, Chirikov, for everything he did. The polling of the crews was nothing new in the Russian Navy; it was the usual practice and commanders were used to it. Bering respected Chirikov and could get along with him, but having to look for approval to the Academicians, who hated him and had used him badly, was a touch that galled him.

Even before this order was out, a former general by the name of Grigori Pisarev, who had been condemned to death, then reprieved, knouted and exiled to Siberia for his part in an abortive palace revolution, had been appointed Commander of the port of Okhotsk and sent off to organize matters there. He was to take Russians and Tunguses from various places in Siberia and settle them around Okhotsk and Yudoma Cross, to cultivate the soil and take care of flocks of sheep, horses and cattle that he would bring in, collect 300 strong young convicts from Yakutsk, take twenty ship carpenters with him from Russia to build four or six ships, and a number of iron workers to smelt iron and forge anchors and other gear.

On December 28, 1732, the Senate issued the final instructions for the Expedition. It was long and detailed.

1- The Senate approves of the expedition in the hope that it will really be for the benefit and glory of Russia. It has given orders to the governor of Siberia, the vice-governor at Irkutsk, and to Pisarev to assist Bering. It is sending members from the Academy of Sciences, students from Moscow, assayers from Ekaterinburg, mechanics and others. It confirms the project to examine not only the waters between Kamchatka and Japan, Kamchatka and America, but also the waters along the Arctic coast.

2- In the instructions which Peter gave to Bering it was evident that Peter desired to determine whether Asia and America were united. Bering says that he went as far as 67° north and found no connection between the two continents. It may be that north and west of the mouth of the Kolyma the two continents do not join, but no one knows whether this is so or not. In order to settle the relation between Asia and America the Admiralty proposes to send exploring expeditions along the Arctic shores from Archangel to the mouth of the Kamchatka River.

3- It has been reported that opposite the mouth of the Kolyma River there is a large land, that Siberians have been on it, and have seen the inhabitants. It is ordered that Bering investigate this matter very thoroughly when he is at Yakutsk. If this is a true report, he should send a sloop to investigate. If it is found that Siberia really joins America so that it is impossible to proceed to Kamchatka, then the investigating party should follow the newly found coast as far as it can to learn in which direction it runs and return to Yakutsk.

If people are found there, they should be treated kindly; they are to be given presents; they are to be asked the extent of their country and its resources, and they are to be invited to become our subjects and to pay tribute. If they are unwilling to do so, they are to be let alone; and no time should be wasted in arguing with them.

It is not at all likely, but it is possible, that by following the Arctic coast our explorers may come to some European settlement. In that case they should act in accordance with the instructions given to Bering and Chirikov. If the explorers ascertain that Siberia and America are not connected, they should proceed to Kamchatka.

5- In regard to going to America, it was ordered in 1731 that ships for this voyage should be built in Okhotsk. If they are ready Bering should take two of them and proceed; if they are not finished, he should finish them. If they have not yet been started on, or if they are not seaworthy, the Admiralty College is of the opinion that the ships should not be built at Okhotsk. Bering recommends that Kamchatka, because it has more timber and a better harbor, should be selected as the place for shipbuilding. Bering desires to have two ships for the voyage so that in case of a misfortune to one of them the other would stand by. If one ship is completed at Okhotsk, it would be a good plan to take that one and go to the Kamchatka River and there build the other one. Bering is to be in command of one of these vessels and Chirikov the other one. On the voyage they are to keep together, work together, and do all that is in their power to advance naval science. To help them a member of the Academy of Sciences (Louis Delisle de la Croyere) is sent along.

6- A late report of Captain Pavlutski, which was sent from Kamchatka, stated that recently Afanase Melnikov with a small party returned from Chukchi Cape. This Melnikov was sent from Yakutsk in 1725 to bring the Chukchi under subjection and make them pay tribute. Melnikov says that in April 1730, while he was on Chukchi Cape, there came over from an island in the sea two men who had pieces of walrus ivory in their lips. These men told Melnikov that it takes a day to go from Chukchi Cape to their island and from there to another island ahead of them, which island is called Large Country. On this Large Country all sorts of animals may be had: sables, beavers, land otters and wild deer. All kinds of green trees grow there. There are many natives on the Large Country; some of them have deer and others have not. Although such reports cannot be trusted, yet they should be followed up and a voyage should be made in the direction of the islands. If they are located and people found on them, they should be treated as instructions in article 4 indicate. Go on from there to America and learn whether there is any continent, or islands, between Kamchatka and America; for, aside from the information furnished by Pavlutski, little is known of the subject. On the map of Professor Delisle a sea is located between Kamchatka and the Spanish province of Mexico in latitude 45 N. If the American coast is discovered, Bering should carry out the instructions given him by Peter in 1725, that is to say, go to some European settlement. If a European ship is met with, he should learn from it the name of the coast, write it down, make a landing, obtain some definite information, draw a map and return to Kamchatka. Be always on your guard not to fall into a trap and not to show the people you meet the way back to Kamchatka.

9- Bering is to take with him 2,000 rubles worth of presents to be distributed among the natives. Chinese tobacco, known as "shar log" is especially worth while because the natives are eager for it.

11- In these voyages search should be made for good harbors and for forests where timber for shipbuilding is to be had. Let mineralogists with a guard go ashore and prospect. If precious minerals are found in some place under Russian jurisdiction, the commander of Okhotsk and the principal officers elsewhere should be notified, and they shall send ships, miners, workmen, instruments, machinery, and provisions and begin working the mines.

12- Geodesists should be sent to examine all the rivers that fall into Lake Baikal from the east in order to find a nearer way to Kamchatka than by Yakutsk.

13- Captain Bering and all the officers in command of ships at sea should keep secret the instructions from the Admiralty College. For Bering, Chirikov, Spanberg and the officers in command of the sloop which is to go east of the Lena to Kamchatka, special instructions are issued and these may be made public. These public instructions are to state that at the request of the St. Petersburg, Paris and other academies the Emperor Peter the Great, of eternal and deserving fame, sent, out of curiosity, an expedition along his own shores to determine whether Asia and America are united. But the expedition did not settle that point. Now Your Imperial

Majesty, influenced by the same reason, is ordering a similar expedition and for a similar purpose. If you should come to settlements under European or Asiatic governments, and are asked the object of your voyage, you may tell them what has just been said. If they demand to see your instructions, show them. This will allay their suspicions, because it is well known that European powers have sent out expeditions and that the question whether Asia and America are united is still unanswered.

14- In order that the expedition may not be retarded on account of delay in getting provisions and supplies of one kind and another, the Admiralty College should send at once special officers to Yakutsk to build boats and expedite the transportation of materials.

15- Because the expedition is harder and farther than any that have ever preceded it, will not Your Majesty reward with money all those who participate in it and give them double pay during the time that they are engaged, promote to the rank of sub-lieutenant the geodesists who have formerly been in Siberia, and to the rank of ensign those who go there for the first time? All officers should receive, either here or in Moscow, a year's pay in advance and, if they desire it, another year's pay in advance either at Tobolsk or Yakutsk, so that they may get their outfits and depart in a contented frame of mind. Bering should arrange with the governor of Siberia and the vice-governor at Yakutsk how the men are to be paid after that.

16- Louis Delisle de la Croyere, at the recommendation of the Academy, is to have charge of the astronomical, physical and other scientific observations of that nature. He is to have two geodesists to help him, Simeon Popov and Andrei Krasilnikov, who have been studying in the St. Petersburg Academy . . .

Bering called his officers together, showed them the instructions, swore them to secrecy in accordance with Article 13, and issued them all copies of the false instructions they were to show on demand if they got into foreign territory. There was a festive air about the proceedings, for they were all drawing down a year's pay, doubled, in advance, and most of them intended to make good use of the money before they left; Chirikov and Spanberg, who had got little out of the First Expedition except well-merited promotions, were pleased by this generous treatment and by the implication that their labors this time were going to be made less onerous. They all had a feeling of belonging to a sort of elite company, being attached to such an important enterprise, and their spirits were high.

It was decided that Chirikov would command the other ship to go to America; Spanberg would command the branch of the Expedition heading for Japan; a Lieutenant Dimitri Ovtsuin was to manage the mapping of the Ob and the Arctic coast on both sides of its mouth, and a Lieutenant Peter Lassinius was to take care of the Lena and the Arctic coast east from its mouth to Kamchatka. The Academy section would act as a sort of commission, moving more or less independently as the learned professors saw fit, with the exception of De la Croyere, who would accompany Chirikov to America. Most of the officers had their doubts about De la Croyere; he was a brother of the Delisles, but had taken his mother's maiden name *because* he was usually in trouble owing to drunkenness and debt. He was not a very good astronomer, and had got his appointment through the intercession of his brother Nicolas; Bering didn't want him, but decided that it would be easier to accept and then more or less ignore him than to quarrel with the Academy again.

The final arrangements and plans were made, and on February 1, 1733, Spanberg got his command together and left St.

Petersburg for Okhotsk, where he was to finish up the ships that Pisarev had been ordered to begin building. He looked forward to a good journey, eased at the most difficult places where Pisarev would have supplies, buildings and help ready for him, but he soon found that he had been rather too optimistic. As he moved along over the same route that the First Expedition had taken he began to hear a great deal of talk about the general worthlessness of Pisarev. The farther he went, the more he found out that this talk was true. Pisarev had done nothing; Pisarev had gathered no mechanics, no native labor, no herds of cattle or anything else. At Yudoma Cross, between Yakutsk and Okhotsk, where the going got very bad and where he had had trouble before, he got into trouble again because he had expected supplies and had sent none forward. Winter caught him again, and the only reason he got his command through was because Lieutenant Sven Waxell, a new but very good man who was to be Bering's second in command later, had got to Yakutsk and managed by Herculean efforts to reach him with enough in the way of supplies.

When he finally got to Okhotsk, two long years after he had left St. Petersburg, he found the same gloomy little village that he had left years before. Pisarev was not to be found, nor were cattle, iron workers, ship carpenters or even buildings to accommodate his force. He had to turn to and build a town before he could even think of starting the construction of his ships. If he had managed to carry any of the optimism of the start that far, he lost it at the first sight of Okhotsk.

Several other parties left after Spanberg had gone from St. Petersburg, but Bering didn't get away with the remainder of his complement until March 18. The Admiralty, shilly-shallying about final instructions, had held him up, finally deciding to let him build ships in Kamchatka if he thought it best. They also, under the prodding of the Academy, impressed upon him the importance of searching for Gamaland and Companyland. He took his wife and daughter with him, and was allowed two servants; several other officers took their families with them.

He reached Tobolsk and then had to spend the rest of the summer and fall waiting for his supplies to catch up with him and building *Tobol*, the two-master that was to be used to chart the Ob and the western Siberian coast. The new officers had had a taste of Siberia and Siberian travel by that time, and had lost some of the enthusiasm of the start; they were to lose more. Ovtsuin and *Tobol* got off down the Ob the following May, after the ice went out, and with the first part of the Arctic-coast mapping program under way, Bering set out eastward again. He reached Yakutsk, over 3000 miles from home, in October. It was getting cold, and he found that no provision whatever had been made for him.

It had become increasingly evident as he traveled, fighting his way through the great swamps and up and down the rivers as before, that despite threats of court martial and torture he was going to get less help from the local authorities the farther he got from St. Petersburg; Yakutsk showed him, if he needed any more showing by that time, that he had got far enough to get no help at all. There had been continual trouble with labor. The natives and the exiled convicts that were to be provided along the way either were not provided by the local authorities or deserted in such numbers that rows of gallows had to be erected along the way to intimidate them.

Yakutsk, that bleak and uncomfortable subarctic town, the coldest in Siberia, was very important to him as a staging area and main depot for the most difficult part of the trip ahead. He needed all the assistance he could get, but the local government, over whom he had no real authority, stayed out of sight and out of reach, cursing him and the government at home for bringing down on them such a locust swarm of incomprehensible people who, by requisitioning everything in sight, threatened them with famine, upset their lives, drafted all the natives they could find at a time when the natives should be getting in the hay for the winter, and interfered beyond bearing with their profitable conniving to steal most of the furs they were collecting for taxes. Some of the Expedition's people went into fur trading themselves and further confused the situation, and drunken fights, murders and other troubles increased in astronomical progression. The bureaucrats lay low, took refuge in the bottle and made what added difficulties their ingenuity could invent.

Despite all this, Bering set to work; in six months after he reached Yakutsk, during the subarctic winter, he managed to construct warehouses, barracks, an iron foundry, a rope walk, two large river boats and four barges to go up the Lena and map the eastern Arctic coast. As soon as travel opened up in the spring of 1735, Chirikov, who had been manhandling the bulk of the supplies across the country, appeared with many more people and further confounded the old inhabitants of the town who had thought they were already terribly put upon. But even more was to be revealed to them; presently the Academy section, which hadn't left St. Petersburg until the summer of 1733, began to come in and continued to appear until September. There were three professors: De la Croyere, Gerhard Müller (who had gone out of his way to give Bering a bad time when he returned from the First Expedition), and Georg Gmelin, who later won fame as a botanist. They had six student secretaries, two artists, an interpreter, a surgeon, an instrument maker, five surveyors and fourteen soldiers who acted as guards when they were sober enough, the labor force to move all these people and several hundred horses. They also had, among other things, several hundred scientific books, a fine supply of lighter literature, nine cartloads of instruments including telescopes up to fifteen feet long, twenty-seven barometers, their provisions, a great store of delicacies and plenty of assorted wines for the professors whose dignity required several varieties with each meal.

Now that they were all—except Spanberg's detail at Okhotsk—gathered together along with the natives who had been impressed into service, the tally ran close to 2000 people—an insane number to be dropped into a bleak place like Yakutsk, which could just about feed itself in pre-Expedition days. With the supplies and equipment that had come in, and despite the uproar that all the new people created, Bering managed to get the two boats started down the Lena. Now that he had those parts of the Expedition which were to survey the two rivers and the Arctic coast out of the way, he could concentrate on the exploration of the Pacific.

All of the great mountain of supplies and equipment to build four sea-going ships at the edge of the known world and maintain them and their crews now had to be transported to Okhotsk over the Stanovoi Mountains and their quaking bogs—the most trackless region of Siberia, the country that had almost killed Spanberg and his people before. As supplies piled up, and the people with it, it began to appear that it was next to impossible to get the affair organized, much less started. The native labor melted away, exiled prisoners escaped and formed roving bands of freebooters, and the bureaucrats of Yakutsk wouldn't do anything about it; Bering's officers, or most of them, got drunk, quarreled among themselves, disappeared for long stretches, countermanded one another's orders and sided first with one faction and then another. The scientists demanded everything they could think of, schemed and maneuvered to get better quarters, for they had arrived after the naval men and had to take what poor accommodations they could get in a town of wretched accommodations; they couldn't do their work in dark and smoky shacks and complained continually, although everyone was fed up with them, out of patience with their pretensions, and paid them no attention. After the way they had treated Bering in St. Petersburg, it is small wonder that he wasn't sympathetic toward them.

Things went from bad to worse, confusion was compounded, and the special mail carriers supplied the Expedition carried little back to St. Petersburg except charges and countercharges. As few people did any work, Bering had to try to do it all. Many of the complaints later that Bering was too lenient in his discipline arose during this time, but if he had been brutal enough to straighten out such a condition, under the existing conditions, he would have come close to depopulating that part of Siberia. He wasted his time and his strength trying to do what his lower officers and petty officers should have done, and worked like a madman while things fell apart around him. It was a time when his limited authority, forced on him at the start, showed up the most.

At the end of four years, when he had planned to be at sea, he was still in Yakutsk; the enterprise had cost 300,000 rubles as opposed to an estimated budget of 12,000, and even the Imperial cabinet realized that the Siberian people had been burdened until they were close to the breaking point. The Cabinet requested the Admiralty to look into the situation and the Admiralty naturally fell upon Bering; they blamed him for everything and cut his pay in half from the beginning of 1738 until after the middle of 1740. That they had some afterthoughts about their treatment of him is shown by orders issued during that time by the Admiralty which threatened various local authorities with torture unless they gave Bering more assistance, and by the appointment—in 1739, six years after the Expedition had started—of several special officers responsible to the Crown and with more authority than had been granted to Bering, to take charge of getting the supplies to Okhotsk and relieve the Captain Commander of this chore. These special officers had been recommended in Article 14 of the Senate's instructions of 1732, but the Admiralty had either overlooked them or simply not bothered to do anything about them.

Bering was not there when they arrived. He was now fifty-eight years old, and had been so worn down and frustrated that he had thrown up his hands and moved his headquarters to Okhotsk to get away from Yakutsk before he went mad; further, he wanted to supervise the construction of his two ships and see how Spanberg was making out with the construction of the ships that would take him to Japan. He found that Okhotsk had increased greatly in size since the First Expedition. Spanberg had built an entire town, picked out the east side of the sandspit where the two rivers joined for his shipbuilding and finished his own ships. He had been unable to sail because he didn't have enough supplies; he had turned to Bering's ships and done some work on them while he waited, but they were far from finished. He had been badly slowed down by lack of materials and by the obstructions put in his way by Pisarev, who had finally appeared and was as energetic as ever in making a nuisance of himself. Spanberg had borne him for a while, although not quietly; finally he got so enraged by Pisarev's machinations that at first he threatened to kill him on sight, and then went after him either to kill him or lock him up. At this, Pisarev fled to Yakutsk.

He was gone by the time Bering arrived in Okhotsk. Bering gave Spanberg what supplies he had managed to get across the mountains for himself, and Spanberg got off in the summer of 1738. He had been in Okhotsk a little over three years.

Having got Spanberg, the last of the supplemental commanders, out of the way, Bering could turn to his own affairs. He made little progress on his ships for a time, working on them into 1739 when the two Crown officers got to Yakutsk and managed to get the transport operation moving. Thereafter he had more to work with, and the construction speeded up. While the work went on he singled out a first mate named Ivan Yelagin, a trustworthy man, and prepared to send him to Avacha Bay, a splendid harbor they had seen on the First Expedition, over 300 miles south of the mouth of the Kamchatka River which had been used the first time. Avacha Bay, being more suitable, had been picked as the staging point this time, and Yelagin was to build a headquarters, barracks and warehouses there in preparation for the arrival of Bering's ships the next year. There was a difficulty in that there was no decent ship to take him to Avacha Bay, but this difficulty was settled when Spanberg returned in August 1739 from his trip to Japan. One of Spanberg's ships had been the old *St. Gabriel*, which had been used on the First Expedition, and it was turned over to Yelagin.

Spanberg had had, in the main, a successful trip. He had visited most of the Kuriles and mapped them pretty well in view of the rain, fog and treacherous currents around them; he had searched for and failed to find Gamaland; and he had made a landing in Japan. He had carried out his orders and would have done more if scurvy hadn't broken out among his crews and killed thirteen of them and if one of his lieutenants, in command of one of the ships, hadn't disobeyed his orders, left the fleet, and thus broken it up.

Spanberg had conceived the notion of inducing the authorities to let him take the expedition out again to subjugate the Kuriles, collect tribute from the islanders, and thus extend the Empire all the way to Japan. He included this idea in his report to Bering; but Bering had learned caution from his dealings with the Admiralty and refused to assume responsibility for it. He called a meeting of all his available officers, where it was agreed to give Spanberg leave to go to St. Petersburg and lay his plans before the Admiralty himself. Accordingly, Spanberg left for Russia; but when he reached Yakutsk he found an order there forbidding him to come any farther. The delay in communications had betrayed him; the Admiralty was preparing to discipline him, as it had disciplined Bering for the events of 1738.

In the meantime, Bering had sent his report to St. Petersburg. It reached the capital in January 1740 and caused a good deal of excitement because it embodied the news of the discovery of the route to Japan. An order was sent to Spanberg to rush to St. Petersburg with all possible speed, and so he started off again down the Lena, which was still frozen.

Pisarev, however, had not been idle. Having a score to settle with Spanberg, he wrote to the Senate that Spanberg was lying about his discoveries, and that he had been in Korea and had never seen Japan. The Senate took this up with the Admiralty; and the Admiralty, already dubious about Spanberg, became more dubious still. They gave him no opportunity to defend himself but sent him a new order in April, ordering him not to come to St. Petersburg but to return to Okhotsk and repeat his Japanese journey. The order caught Spanberg in Ustkutsk in July, and sent him cursing back toward the Pacific again. It said nothing about subjugating the Kuriles; he was merely to repeat the trip he had made once. When he reached Yudoma Cross he caught up with Georg Wilhelm Steller, a remarkable man who was on his way to join Bering, and the two of them traveled together to Okhotsk.

It would be well to break the narrative here and introduce Steller, for his knowledge would have been invaluable during the trip to America if he could have got anyone to listen to him. His trouble was that he was an intellectual, scornful of the opinions of anyone not so well educated as himself, and all too liable to show his scorn. He had too much to say, particularly to sailors, whom he considered stupid and ignorant, and was not in the least tactful in saying it. He knew nothing of the sea but was always ready to hand out advice about how to cope with it; consequently, it was not long before any advice he gave, good or bad, was ignored.

He was a Franconian, born in Windsheim in 1709 of a good family, an intelligent boy who always stood at the head of his class in school. He was restless, energetic, inquisitive and fearless; early in life he became much interested in natural history, and after his early schooling he went to the University of Wittenburg and then to Halle on a scholarship to teach botany. He studied medicine while he taught, but as there was no chair of botany at

Halle to support him after the scholarship ran out, he had to find something else to do.

Catherine had founded the Academy by that time, turned over an imposing palace to it and given it a yearly subsidy of 25,000 rubles. Many Germans were going to Russia to work there; it seemed to promise wider opportunities than the rather crowded, settled academic scene in Germany, and Steller decided to try his luck. He went to Danzig, the closest point of entry. He was well received by the Russians, who were short of doctors, and assigned as a medical advisor to an artillery regiment. They couldn't make him a doctor because he had no degree. When the regiment went to St. Petersburg, he went with them.

Luckily, he met the Archbishop Theophan after he had been in the capital for a short time, and Theophan took a liking to him; he appointed Steller his companion and household physician. Theophan was an important man; he had been a friend of Peter's and had conducted Peter's funeral service. He was reforming public education, which was extremely poor in Russia, and editing the new Ecclesiastical regulations. He had the best library in Russia and a number of friends in the Academy to whom he recommended Steller, and Steller soon had the run of the place. He spent a good deal of time there when he was not with Theophan or botanizing in the country near St. Petersburg, for the Academy had a fine library by this time, a collection of miscellaneous curiosities which had been started by Peter, a bookstore and a printing office. There was a school attached to it, but when it had been started there were no young men to attend it because the educational level of the country had been so low. Finally a few young men who knew Latin were rounded up and paid to attend; they were known as adjuncts, but acted as secretaries and assistants, and Steller was put in this classification. Most of the Academicians were Germans, who were still arrogant and supercilious toward the Russians who surrounded them. The Russians were suspicious of their foreign tricks, and the westerners living in St. Petersburg thought them too theoretical and not interested enough in the practical sciences. No one really liked them, but the Academicians paid little attention to what anyone thought; they bickered and squabbled among themselves and went their own sweet way. The atmosphere wasn't one to teach humility to a young man who had none of his own, which was unfortunate; it would have helped him later.

The Academy was the center of scientific life and activity in the capital, which had a population of about 100,000 when Steller was there. Many palaces and buildings that had been started when Peter was alive were finished now. Some visitors to St. Petersburg found it overwhelming, splendid and grand; Asiatic luxury existed in a city built in a combination of European styles, and there was fine music, opera, theatrical performances, gambling and drinking. A very gay life was lived at Court and in the palaces, but the veneer was thin and manners in the main were still boorish; great ladies, loaded with jewels and dressed in Paris creations, were often seen carrying their shoes, and inasmuch as there were 196 fast days on the calendar, everyone ate and drank prodigious amounts on the days when no fast was in order. One sour Italian nobleman who visited the city remarked on all this and went on to say that walls were cracked and out of plumb and the roofs leaked; elsewhere, he said, ruins become naturally so, but in St. Petersburg they were built that way. It was a city built hurriedly by order, without traditions or history.

The population was as mixed as the architecture. Asia and

Europe met in St. Petersburg; there was a multitude of races, costumes and languages. Everyone spoke several languages but none of them very well; many foreign children brought up there spoke a heterogeneous mixture of Russian, English, French, Swedish, Polish and Finnish.

This was the St. Petersburg in which young Steller found himself, but he didn't mix in the social life. He was poor, and studious, and busy studying and botanizing in 1735, when there was a good deal of talk about the Expedition. The Academicians decided that Müller and Gmelin were to go with Bering to explore Siberia and Kamchatka, and then thought that these two should be reinforced by two more men. Steller had always had a burning inclination toward exploration and adventure, and it was aroused to a fever pitch by all the talk. He asked Theophan to recommend him for one of the two openings. This Theophan did; and although he died in 1736, his influence was great enough to insure Steller's appointment. To Steller's great satisfaction, he finally got his orders to go to Kamchatka; he was sure that he could talk Bering into taking him to America when he met the great man, and he was confident that he could get his orders from the Academy changed once Bering had expressed an interest in him. Great things seemed to be opening up before him: lands no one had ever seen, new flora and fauna, a chance to make a lasting name for himself.

chapter
seven

WITH SPANBERG ON his way to St. Petersburg and the supplies
coming in well under the direction of the Crown officers, Bering
was able to push the construction of his ships through the winter
of 1739 and the spring of 1740. In June the ships left the stocks.
They were alike, each 80 feet long, with a beam of 22 feet and a
draft of 9½ feet; they had two masts, brig-rigged, fourteen two-
and three-pounder cannon, and could carry a burden of 110 tons.
They were named *St. Peter* and *St. Paul;* Bering decided upon
St. Peter as his flagship, and Chirikov took over command of *St.
Paul.*

According to the Admiralty's plan, the Expedition was to winter
in America after it got there, spending two years on the trip. This
would necessitate spending the winter of 1740–41 at Avacha Bay
in Kamchatka to get as early a start as possible in the summer of
1741, and would require an enormous amount of provisions.
There was little to eat in Kamchatka but fish, and as they had
found out in Okhotsk, a steady fish diet was not satisfactory; it
constipated most of the men and made some of them sick after a
while. The entire supply of ships' biscuit for the two-year trip
had also been baked in Okhotsk while they had been there. All

of the biscuit and the rest of the provisions had to be transported
to Avacha Bay, and there was a shortage of ships; only one of
Spanberg's fleet was available. Bering had to supplement his
supply flotilla by borrowing a galiot that had been built for the
local government and tax gatherers of Okhotsk.

It had been his plan to get away from Okhotsk on August 12,
but just before that date Spanberg and Steller, who had been
traveling together, appeared. Spanberg had his orders with him
to take the Japanese Expedition out again, and threw everything
into confusion. Bering had loaded all available provisions and supplies on his ships and had to unload enough of them to supply
Spanberg until he could get enough of his own from Yakutsk,
which meant rooting about and disturbing all his own loading
arrangements and ships' trim; and conferences and meetings had
to be held to plan Spanberg's new expedition. Spanberg himself
had to be smoothed down, for he was still simmering with rage
and frustration about Pisarev and his new orders, and was inclined
to express himself in a very lively fashion. The delay enabled a
courier from St. Petersburg—where the French ambassador was
trying to stir up a war between Russia and the Swedes and encouraging Peter's daughter Elizabeth to unseat Ivan VI, who had
succeeded Anna—to appear with orders from the Admiralty for
Bering to submit a new, full report of his plans for his own expedition. In the midst of all these tribulations Bering said good-by to
his wife and daughter and saw them off to St. Petersburg and met
Steller, who both amused and impressed him. He suggested that
Steller might like to go with the Expedition as mineralogist, and
Steller, without giving a definite answer, implied that he would
like to think about this. Bering didn't press the matter, for he was
preoccupied at the moment. To his harassed mind the order for

a report was another criticism and intimation of the Admiralty's dissatisfaction, particularly after the way they had treated Spanberg.

He was disturbed enough by the order to be hurried into a decision to send a ship, loaded with all the biscuit and some other supplies, ahead of the fleet to Avacha, under the command of one of his lieutenants, named Sofron Khitrov. He did this to show some evidence of progress in the new report, but he had never seen Khitrov handle a ship. It was probably one of the most unfortunate decisions he ever made; for although Khitrov had talked well enough about ship handling during the overland journey, he turned out to be a poor sailor. Before he was out of the river's mouth he ran the ship aground on one of the sand bars that were continually shifting about in the lower river, and holed her. She filled with water; all of the ships' biscuit and most of the other supplies were ruined, and the ship had to be patched, refloated and towed in for repairs, so that it was not until September 8 that the fleet got under way.

The loss of time and the extra work were the crowning irritations in a long, long series of irritations, but the loss of the biscuit was a great disaster. It was too late to replace it without postponing the departure to Avacha for another year, and that, considering the evident impatient state of mind of the Admiralty and the Senate, was impossible; and because the biscuit was lost and irreplaceable, the plans for wintering in America had to be dropped. The complexion of the Expedition changed. Instead of having plenty of time in front of him, Bering now was faced with a terrible uncertainty and knew that he would have to get to America and back in a single summer. He didn't know how far he would have to go, how long the trip out would take and, not knowing the weather conditions at the end of summer when he would be returning, how long would be required for the return. He knew now that he would be rushed and apprehensive during the entire trip, that he would never be able to forget the problem of his return for a moment, and a shadow was laid on his weary and overburdened mind which he never shook off.

The four-ship fleet reached the mouth of the Bolshaya, on the western shore of Kamchatka, on September 21. The low, swampy coast, with its shifting sand bars and shoals, was as dreary as ever and nothing could be seen ashore but a few dilapidated sheds. Steller and De la Croyere, who had made the trip in the galiot *Okhotsk,* one of the two supply ships that were both going to unload at Bolsheretsk because they weren't considered sound enough to sail around the peninsula and into the Pacific at that time of year, decided to go on to Bolsheretsk and spend the winter there. Bering was of no mind to risk his two ships by hanging about on that flat and tricky coast in September, and left the next day. Yelagin, who had come over from Avacha Bay and his construction work to meet Bering, went with him.

St. Peter almost came to disaster doubling Cape Lopatka, at the southern end of the peninsula. There was a channel about five miles wide and several miles long between Lopatka and the most northerly of the Kuriles, with a rocky reef running down the middle of it; *St. Peter* steered into the northern channel with a stiff west wind behind her and heavy seas running. They had no tide tables for this place; the tide was running west, and in the turbulent water running against the wind the ship was caught and held almost stationary for an hour or so with waves breaking over her stern and either side. The ship's boat, which they were towing, was smashed against the stern, and the waves were so high that Waxell (who later wrote that he had never been in such peril in a life of seafaring) estimated that there was no more than three fathoms of water under them when they were in the troughs. The wind increased so much while they were in this position that they were afraid they would lose what sails they were carrying, but they couldn't reef them and still keep St. Peter's bow to the seas; they would have been swamped if they had tried to come about. They managed to keep the ship's head to the seas until the tide slowed, and then began to move. An hour and a half later, when Chirikov came through the channel, he had no trouble at all; he missed the frightening example of what tide and wind could do in the Kuriles.

Once around Lopatka, they changed course up the high and mountainous coast. On the twenty-seventh they were near Avacha, but fog and storms drove them out to sea. The damaged ship's boat was lost in the foul weather, and it wasn't until October 6 that they sailed into Avacha Bay and on to their winter harbor, which had been christened Petropavlovsk. Chirikov was already there, having arrived on September 27, and Khitrov, who was bringing the ship he had almost wrecked once, didn't appear at all. He had been unable to double Cape Lopatka and had damaged his ship, almost losing her. He had to limp back to Bolsheretsk, where the supplies that were unloaded there from his ship were stored to be hauled across Kamchatka when winter set in—a state of affairs that caused a great deal of trouble later on. One wonders why Bering had left him in command, after his performance at Okhotsk, except that all the new officers were untried at sea, anyone can have trouble with a shifting sand bar, and Bering's mind was bedeviled enough to have some effect upon his judgment of a man.

Avacha Bay is one of the best natural harbors in the world, and one of the most beautiful. It is nearly eleven miles in diameter, with a well-protected entrance, a uniform depth averaging twelve fathoms, and no hazards to navigation. The hills surrounding it are covered with birch woods and luxurious vegetation, and to the north a group of magnificent volcanoes thrust up their snowy cones into the sky for 11,000 feet or more. The bay freezes over in winter and is frozen until April or May, but ice cannot be avoided on the east coast of Kamchatka; and for once the Expedition found fine quarters waiting for it. Yelagin had done very well; he had picked a good location at the head of the best inner harbor and built a little town of good log houses: officers' quarters, barracks for the men, warehouses for the supplies and so on. The natives, Kamchadals, who had been moved in to supply labor had built themselves sod houses. During the winter he was there, Bering had a church built, and travelers who came that way later all remarked upon its beauty. The harbor's name, Petropavlovsk, had come from a combination of the names of the two ships.

After he was settled for the winter and had a little time to organize matters, Bering completed his plans for the Expedition and arranged his crew roster. He decided to make Sven Waxell, who had been second in command from Okhotsk, his first lieutenant, and it was a good choice. Waxell was a Swede who had been born in Stockholm in 1701; a fair-minded and conscientious man who had joined the Russian Navy in 1726. He had proved his worth during the transport operation and was to prove it more as the Expedition went on. He had his minor son with him, a boy named

Lavrentij, probably because the boy had wanted so badly to go and Bering had allowed it.

Khitrov was made the second officer on St. *Peter,* probably because Bering wanted him where he could keep an eye on him and because he thought it would be prudent to have a Russian among his officers. An old, experienced sailor named Eselberg was made first mate, and Kharlan Yushin second mate. Khitrov and Yushin were both to keep logbooks. Chirikov's lieutenants were named Chikhachev and Plautin, and he was to take De la Croyere in his ship. There were seventy-five men in St. *Paul's* complement, and seventy-four in St. *Peter's.*

Mathias Betge, whom he was going to take with him as doctor and surgeon, fell ill and requested that he be sent back to St. Petersburg, and Bering thought of Steller again. He was sixty years old now, and the sturdy body that had served him so excellently was wearing out. The strain and worry of the four years from the arrival at Yakutsk to the arrival at Petropavlovsk, the constant warfare with Siberian bureaucracy and the attitude of the Admiralty and the Senate, the loss of the ships' biscuit and the consequent change of plans on top of the stresses of the Expedition's start and the first four years on top of that had ground him down. He wasn't feeling at all well and desperately wanted a doctor with him; and although he knew that Steller had no medical degree, he was aware that Steller had read a good deal of medical literature, had had medical experience and was a clever and learned man. Also, he had been instructed by the Admiralty to take a mineralogist with him, and Steller was a mineralogist. Further, he liked Steller for his lively and amusing ways, and Steller had intimated that he would like to go to America. He wrote

Steller at Bolsheretsk in February, and asked him to come across the peninsula for an interview.

Steller had already written to the Academy requesting to be sent with Spanberg on the second trip to Japan, but after getting to Okhotsk and Bolsheretsk and hearing more about the American expedition, he decided he would rather go with Bering; an entirely new country was about to be discovered, and he wanted to be in on the discovery. As soon as he received Bering's note he guessed what was in the wind, and started out for Petropavlovsk. He had had enough of Bolsheretsk, in any event. The town, which had originally been a small palisaded fort and a few houses built by the Cossacks, had grown after the First Expedition. The normal garrison was forty-five soldiers, who collected taxes and traded with the natives for furs, and a few officials who extorted money from anyone they could push around. When the Second Expedition had settled and the population had skyrocketed, there was an acute housing shortage, what with the merchants who had gathered, the new people and the officials, messengers and so on who came and went from St. Petersburg. The sailors had turned petty traders and ruined the Cossack's fur market; the officers, who had discovered a number of promissory notes in Yakutsk signed by people in Bolsheretsk, had bought these notes up and foreclosed on them when they reached Bolsheretsk. They swung cat-o'-nine-tails on everyone who didn't jump to obey their orders, and even common soldiers grew very inflated in their opinions of themselves; there was a local proverb to the effect that a private in Moscow began acting like a sergeant in Tobolsk, an ensign in Tomsk, a lieutenant on the Lena, a captain in Yakutsk and a colonel in Kamchatka. The local vodka distillery couldn't keep up with the demand, the trapping season had been very bad and few sables had been caught; and between that, the thieving officials and the officers' demands for payment on the foreclosed notes, everybody in town was broke and disgruntled.

The only way to get across the peninsula at that time of year was by dog sled, and it would have been better to wait until March or April when the snow was hard and the weather milder, but Steller wasn't inclined to wait. He set off, over the trackless mountains and through the equally trackless willow jungles, which were always ready to break one's arms or legs or scratch out one's eyes; the dogs ran away several times; a storm came up and Steller had to hole up under the overturned sled until it blew itself out. The distance was only about 140 miles, but it took him ten days to do it. He was impressed by the cleanness of Petropavlovsk and the beauty of the country.

When he got in to see Bering, he realized very quickly that he had an advantage: Bering, tired and unwell, was as anxious to have him as he was anxious to go. He put on an air of reluctance, saying that his assignment from the Academy was to explore Kamchatka; in fact, he had already written to the Academy, asking them if he could go with Spanberg instead of staying where he was. What if this change of assignment was already on the way from St. Petersburg? The Academy would discipline him severely if he disobeyed his instructions.

Bering set about trying to convince him that his work would be the same only more interesting because it would be in a new country; but Steller still appeared to hesitate. He had made an enemy of Khitrov because he had been very outspoken about Khitrov's blunderings, and now Khitrov was second officer of St. Peter, upon which he would be sailing. Also, he required an assistant or two to help with his collections and whatnot. Bering brushed all these difficulties aside. He would arrange for an assistant or two, he said; he would take care of Khitrov. As for the Academy's instructions, he would take care of them, too. He was supreme commander of the Expedition and his orders superseded the Academy's. He promised to call a meeting of his officers, a soviet, and have Steller's new instructions written up and signed by all of them.

Steller now had everything he wanted; he agreed to go with the Expedition. That done, he joined the Easter celebrations being held around the harbor; after sobering up several days later, he spent his time writing to everyone he could think of in St. Petersburg to suggest changes and improvements in the way Kamchatka should be run. There was still six feet of snow covering the country; he couldn't go out on collecting trips, and he had too much vitality to sit still. He was outraged by the ill treatment of the natives, who were exploited at every turn and callously pushed around, the drunkenness and veniality of the government officials and the sad state of the church's affairs, and felt that he should report these things. He also reviewed the medical supplies to be taken on the trip and found them to consist mostly of plasters, ointments and other things more useful for battle wounds than anything else, and complained; there were no antiscorbutics, for instance, which would be of supreme importance on a long sea voyage to stave off scurvy, that scourge of seafarers in those times. His complaints did little good, for the medical chests had been made up in Moscow, and there was nothing to be done about them now.

His ideas were good; they usually were; but, as usual, he showed little restraint or diplomacy in putting them forward. He was clever and logical but headlong and frequently outspokenly sarcastic, impatient with fools in a country that was full of them, and always ready to advise people whether they wanted his advice or not. His advice would have saved much trouble and even lives if he had brought it forward differently.

After the ships were unrigged and snugged down for the winter, the question became one of conserving the sea provisions and getting more in from Bolsheretsk, where they had been unloaded from Khitrov's ship. The command was put on a diet of fish, reindeer meat and half bread rations, most of which could be come by locally, so that there couldn't possibly be a shortage in the ships' supply. Meanwhile, the bulky provisions—amounting to about 180 pounds for every man at Avacha Bay—that Khitrov had had to land because of his second disaster had to be brought across the mountains to Petropavlovsk. There were no horses in Kamchatka at the time, and they couldn't have been used anyhow during the deep snows of the winter months; the freighting had to be done with dog sleds or on men's backs over an extraordinarily difficult country. There weren't enough natives or dogs around Bolsheretsk for this operation; they had to be rounded up for a distance of 300 miles or so, and this took the recruiters into the northern part of Kamchatka where the Koryaks lived. The recruiting was done brutally and inefficiently, for Kolessov, the commander of the garrison, was a drunken and slipshod man, and the Koryaks, who were a tougher people than the Kamchadals, revolted at once because of the harsh treatment they received, because of the fact that many of them had never left their homes and didn't want to, and because they didn't understand the operation, anyhow. The Kamchadals, depressed as they were, revolted after the operation began because of its tremendous difficulties and the way they were handled. Seven or eight Russians were killed and troops were sent out; natives were shot and surprised in their underground houses and had grenades dropped down on them; Bering and his officers had to hold investigations, smooth things over as best they could and start the recruiting all over again. All this took so long that the Expedition was a month late in starting in the spring. It was a time they could ill afford, for the summer season was short in those latitudes and the Expedition's time had already been cut from two years to one by Khitrov's loss of the ships' biscuit at Okhotsk. All this didn't lighten the burdens already being borne by the Captain Commander.

Khitrov began his logbook on April 23, 1741, when the supplies began to go aboard and the work was started on rerigging the ships. The weather was still bad; there was ice in the harbor and snowstorms were not at all unusual, but the work went on. On May 4 there was a snowstorm and there was a council of the officers, and another unfortunate decision was forced upon Bering. De la Croyere had his brother Guillaume's instructions to find Gamaland; the Academy had backed these instructions when Bering had been given his final orders; and so they had to find it. The council finally agreed, with great reluctance, to lay their course southeast by east to the forty-sixth parallel. They also ratified the decision forced upon them by Khitrov's clumsiness, to return to Petropavlovsk in September, and discussed the advisability of sailing north to East Cape after the Gamaland search. The Admiralty had suggested that America might be closer to Siberia there, and a number of people in Bolsheretsk were of the same opinion. But Bering was skeptical; he had seen nothing to support this view on the First Expedition. The final decision was that it was too early to go very far north; after hunting for Gamaland and discovering America by sailing eastward, they would turn north to latitude 65° or so and return home by way of East Cape, finding then whether it was close to America or not.

The loading of the belated supplies and the fitting of the ships were finally finished; the crews went aboard on May 22. There were seventy-eight men on *St. Peter's* roster, including Lieutenant Waxell's son and Steller, who was given a bunk in Bering's cabin; *St. Paul's* roster held seventy-six men, including De la Croyere. On the twenty-fourth, Sunday, Bering hoisted his flag on *St. Peter;* he inspected the crews of both ships on the next day, and received cheers from both crews. There was a cold rain falling but no wind, and Bering and Chirikov agreed upon an elaborate signal code to be used between the two ships.

Now that they were ready, the wind failed them; it gave no indication of blowing for four days. At four o'clock on the morning of the twenty-ninth a light breeze sprang up, bringing a promise of more wind to come. Bering had a gun fired on *St. Peter* as a signal for church services on both ships, to invoke God's blessing on their enterprise. The breeze soon dropped, however, and finally both ships were towed out of the inner harbor into the open roadstead, where they anchored. Presently the wind came up again, but unfavorably, and veered about until four o'clock in the morning of June 4, when it steadied from the northwest. Anchors were weighed; the fore-topsails and the fore-topmast staysails were hoisted on both ships, and by 9:00 A.M. under these sails they were negotiating the narrow entrance from Avacha Bay to the sea.

They were clear and away by noon, with all sails except

the spritsails set, on an east-southeast course. Their landmark and first meridian was a lighthouse that Bering had built at the mouth of the bay. The coast of Kamchatka and the three snowy volcanoes to the north slowly faded from sight as the afternoon waned and dusk fell, and the stars brightened over the immense empty disc of the sea.

They were away for the New World and whatever adventures the seeking would bring them, after eight years. All Siberia hoped never to see them again. Lassenius and most of the men they had sent with him down the Lena to explore the Arctic coast were dead of scurvy in the north, and Ovtsuin, who they had sent down the Ob from Tobolsk, had failed, been degraded in rank and was on *St. Peter* with them. Only Spanberg, of all the branch expeditions, had done what he had set out to do; and the Admiralty and Senate hadn't accepted his discoveries because of Pisarev's vengeful lies.

Their plan was to hold the southeast-by-east course enforced on them as far as latitude 46° north, and, if Gamaland hadn't been sighted by then, to change course to east and east by north. If they had held this course from the beginning, as all the officers had wanted to do, they would have reached the American coast in eight days. The inventions of the great Delisle, backed by the Academy, prevented that and caused them much trouble. Waxell, writing of the voyage forty years after he returned from it, said of Gamaland and Delisle's map: "I know that I am writing all too much of this matter but I can hardly tear myself away from it, for my blood still boils whenever I think of the scandalous deception of which we were the victims."

chapter
eight

Now THAT THEY were well at sea and all of the grinding worry
that had been Bering's portion for the eight years since he had
left St. Petersburg, all of the delays and frustrations and troubles
that the 6000 miles of the transport operation had piled upon his
aging body and overtried nervous system—as well as the tensions
he had experienced before the Second Expedition was decided
upon—caught up with him. The ships were away at last; he had
got them started in spite of everything that circumstances and
men could do. The die was cast, no courier from the Admiralty
could change it, and all was in the hand of God; and suddenly
the nervous energy that had held him up through the long years
was gone. It had lasted astonishingly well, carrying him through
the swamps of western Siberia, down the Lena, through the four
nightmare years at Yakutsk, across the Stanovoi Mountains to
Okhotsk and the time there; the disastrous clumsiness of Khitrov
and the change of plans for wintering in America. It had sent
off two sub-expeditions to the murderous Arctic coast, and Spanberg twice to Japan; built hundreds of buildings, scores of boats,
a dozen ships; managed and fed 2000 exiles, convicts, natives
and his own people in a world of Russians who hated, envied,

cursed or used him in one way or another. One by one, directly or indirectly, they had made demands upon that energy, and now the reservoir was empty. He went into his cabin and stayed there, as a wounded and exhausted animal goes to its lair.

And now most of the conning of the ship fell upon Waxell, who in his own account of the voyage never complained, although his work was more than doubled. Perhaps he was pleased at this unexpected and unofficial promotion and at the power and responsibility it gave him. He would have been a strange man if it hadn't pleased him, but there is never a word of self-congratulation, or any oblique and slighting reference to his commander, or to the fact that he wasn't paid for the added responsibility that had fallen upon him, or to the extra worry and work, or to the fact that he could earn a great deal of blame but little credit. He never mentioned that Bering had taken to his bed, or spent most of his time in his cabin, or even implied it. He took over, reporting to Bering when there was anything to report, and the search for Gamaland began. It was cold, with the wind coming mostly out of the north; the ships stayed within sight of one another, burning lanterns at night, occasionally moving close to talk. They kept men in the crosstrees in the daytime and took frequent soundings after dark, but found no bottom anywhere at ninety fathoms to indicate that land was near.

This went on until June 12, when they reached 46° north latitude, and still there was no sight of land. The elusive Gamaland remained invisible. At the last conference before sailing they had all agreed to give up the search for this land of Delisle's invention at this latitude. St. Paul was signaled to approach and the ships drew together, pitching in the light wind; Waxell and Chirikov, by use of their speaking trumpets, agreed to call off the search, change course to east-northeast, and sail for America. Eight precious days had already gone into the search for Gamaland, and many more would be used to make up for the distance lost on the old course.

The ships were then at about 174° east longitude; the nearest land to the north was 375 miles away, and to the south and southeast there was nothing closer than New Zealand and the South Pole, but Steller had seen some seaweed floating past the ship during the day and a few ducks and terns, and so he decided that land was near. He fell into argument with the officers, insisting that another day on the old east-southeast course would bring them to a landfall. It was the first time that the officers had seen Steller exercising his omnipotence. He had been an amusing and lively fellow; they had liked him, and, besides, he had Bering's ear, being bunked with the Commander. At first they gave him soft answers and tried to calm him down. But he would have none of it; he grew more heated and then sarcastic, and finally they turned their backs and refused to listen to him. He had had no experience with the sea; but as the superior man, the repository of logic and intelligence, he was much put out by the fact that those whom he considered ignorant sailors wouldn't pay him any attention. He complained at great length in his journal and thereafter looked upon them as fools—a sentiment which they reciprocated with some enthusiasm, and from then on the rift between them widened until they couldn't get together on anything.

The ships stayed on the northeast course until June 20, when bad weather, intermittent fog and a gale of wind caused Chirikov to heave-to under his mizzen. At ten in the morning *St. Paul* failed to reappear. At four *St. Peter* got under way again, looking for her, and kept the neighborhood for two days with the lookouts doubled and a man constantly in the crosstrees. By the twenty-second the officers were greatly concerned, for it had been planned to keep the two ships together as mutual help for one another in the unknown seas they were sailing. There was a conference in Bering's cabin, where it was decided to turn south again to the forty-fifth parallel to take a final look for Gamaland and St. Paul; for it had been agreed that they would each go back to the position where they had lost sight of each other in the event that they became separated. By the twenty-sixth they had passed the forty-sixth degree of latitude without seeing either land or the other ship. They decided to give her up (it had been twenty-one days now since they had left Avacha) and take up their course north and east again. They set off upon it at noon of the twenty-fifth. It was just as well that they wasted no more time looking for St. Paul, for Chirikov had not gone back to the forty-fifth parallel. The two ships had moved around each other for two days, sometimes barely out of sight of one another over the horizon, and then Chirikov had dropped south a degree or so and swung east. On the twenty-fifth he was close to ten degrees of latitude east of them and four degrees of longitude to the north. The ships never sighted one another again.

On their new course the wind stayed southerly and there was considerable fog until July 1, when the wind came around to the north and brought rain and a higher sea. The water supply had begun to run low, and to conserve it and the rations the officers decided that the crew should be cut to mush twice a day. The course was held for nearly two weeks—days of fog and rain with little sunshine. A dead whale floated past and later a piece of driftwood which made them think that land might be near, but bottom couldn't be found at 180 fathoms with the lead. On

July 10, at about fifty-two degrees of latitude, Steller again told them that land was near, although the nearest island was 240 nautical miles away. He made a nuisance of himself about it and even went to Bering, who replied to his arguments that he was being ridiculous and annoying and knew nothing of nautical matters.

By the fourteenth half of the water supply had been consumed and it was not known whether the reserve supply in the lower hold would last until August 25, at which time they had agreed they would start home from the New World; no one was sure that a good deal of it hadn't leaked out of the barrels. They were getting farther from Kamchatka every day and had been at sea without seeing land since June 4; it was time to face the possibility that they would have to come about and return to Kamchatka while they still had water enough to get them there, without discovering anything. The time they had wasted in the futile search for Gamaland and in looking for St. Paul was catching up with them, and there was a mounting tension aboard. America was surely somewhere in front of them, but where? How far? How much longer could they continue looking for it, with their water supply going down and their backlog in the lower hold impossible to estimate before the imminent autumn gales and wintry weather began?

Bering called a conference of the officers in his cabin, and all of these things were considered. Finally they decided to compromise and change course to east-northeast, which would bring them to land—and fresh water—if any existed to the north (as some reports had it), without taking them so far from home as the old course; for they were, in a way, turning on to the vertical leg of a triangle the hypotenuse of which would take them home.

The meeting broke up and the course was changed. The weather was good that day; the wind died out around midnight but came up again, lightly, in the morning. They had been sailing for six weeks now, and everyone was on the stretch; tense expectation and hope held them all, which the change of course seemed to have increased. Toward evening the wind freshened and the sky began to cloud over. Steller had been walking the deck all afternoon, with his gaze on the northern horizon, and before the light began to fail he thought that he saw the dim, indistinct outline of snowy mountains far ahead. His shout brought most of them running to the bow to see the land that had long been their hope. There was an uproarious and sudden pandemonium, brought on by an upsurge of relief from gloomy thoughts of hunger and thirst and the monotony of the cold fogs and the endless empty sea. They chattered and slapped one another's backs, although some said they could see the mountains and some said they could not. The officers presently calmed them down by saying that none of them could see anything and doubted if there was land in the offing, and Steller complained bitterly in his journal that they took this attitude only because it was he who had seen the land. Nevertheless, they heaved the lead several hours later and failed to find bottom at ninety fathoms.

As soon as it was light on the sixteenth, people lined the rail, searching the northern horizon. It was cloudy, with the sun occasionally breaking through the clouds, and the wind was strong enough so that the topsails were reefed. At eleven o'clock the lead was heaved again, and again found no bottom at ninety fathoms. Noon found them in a drizzle of rain, but presently a break in the clouds enabled them to make a solar observation, which showed their position to be 58° 14′ north; and suddenly, at twelve-thirty, the clouds lifted to show them the bleakly magnificent saw-toothed wall of the Alaskan-coast range looming through the mists, capped by the towering 18,000-foot volcanic peak of Mt. St. Elias thrusting its snowy bulk into the sky. Their long uncertainty was over; they had discovered America.

There was great rejoicing on *St. Peter*, and for a while, before going off into his own meditations, Steller enjoyed himself listening to the naïve, excited babble of the crew, the members of which congratulated themselves and each other on their hardihood and skill and the fact that they would now be well rewarded, rich and famous. He was greatly moved, for the new continent opened before him an unparalleled opportunity. He would return to St. Petersburg and glory with collections of plants, minerals and animals that no white man had ever seen before; he thought of long expeditions ashore, and hoped that Bering, now that America had been discovered after such toil and trouble, would spend the winter here despite the lack of food or comfort or even minimum safety. He never thought of the suffering or the deaths it might entail, or the danger; he would survive and never tire in the face of this wonderful opportunity.

It was very different with Bering. When the officers reported the landfall to him and accompanied him up on deck, he stared at the coast for a time and shrugged and turned away. After sixteen years of the greatest hardship and trouble, of suffering and bad luck and ill treatmeant by the Academy and the Admiralty, he stood face to face with the supreme moment of his life, and it had come far too late for him. He was sixty years old; in the last sixteen years his health and his spirit had been broken. His thoughts went back over these years: the First Expedition, when they wouldn't even accept his maps; the Second, the greatest the world had ever known with its enormous responsibilities, when they piled ever more upon him and then hedged his authority about until he had little left. He thought of the future: they were six weeks from home in an unknown ocean, without supplies for the winter, and who knew what winds would soon come up in the autumn season and perhaps hold them there until summer came again?

He felt no triumph at all, only an immense weariness and foreboding. He turned away from men who crowded in to congratulate him, and they stared, nonplussed, and made disgruntled comments behind his back.

By afternoon they were close enough under the shore to see the fine forests marching down to the sea, the coastal plain and the beach. They continued on and, the weather worsening, moved farther out; heavy clouds and rain squalls came down and hid the coast, and it wasn't until the evening of the eighteenth that they encountered land again. It was not the mainland but the seaborne mountain clothed with spruces which is now Kayak Island, and they spent the night tacking across the wind to get behind it and into a temporary anchorage out of the wind. They were still in an unfavorable position on Sunday morning, and spent the rest of the day and the night trying to get into a good one; at six o'clock the next morning they anchored about a mile off shore.

Bering, whose primary interest was a safe anchorage in the event of a blow, ordered Khitrov to take the longboat and look for one in the strait between Kayak and the mainland or among the islands to the north of them, and return as soon as he found such an anchorage. Steller, of course, was wild with impatience to set foot on the New World and requested permission to go with Khitrov. Bering refused it; he wanted Khitrov to get his job done and return. He had found America and established its location; other expeditions, better supplied and able to reach America earlier in the season, could investigate it further; he had to think of stocking up with fresh water and getting his ship and crew home in safety before autumn came down on him.

Steller was almost beside himself, as any scientist would have been in the circumstances. He demanded to know if the only purpose of the Expedition, after ten years of hardship and toil, was merely to take water from America back to Asia. He begged and wheedled and finally threatened Bering, who answered him that the land might be full of bloodthirsty savages who would kill him and that he, Bering, refused to accept the responsibility for it. Steller replied that he had never been a womanish and fearful man; he would take his chances, and his duty to science and the Academy demanded he go ashore at once. Bering was adamant. Khitrov and the long boat shoved off without Steller, whereupon he so far forgot himself as to threaten his commander, before all the crew, with being put on report to the Admiralty and the Senate.

This effrontery, along with the uproar that he had already created, would have landed Steller in irons in the brig on any other ship; but the long-suffering Captain Commander, tacitly acknowledging that there was some justice in Steller's demands, shook off his gloomy forebodings for a while, laughed good-naturedly at him and finally said he could go ashore in the yawl with the watering party at ten o'clock. Hot chocolate, probably the rarest and costliest drink in Europe at the time and certainly the rarest in the North Pacific, was being served in honor of the discovery, but Steller wouldn't wait for it. With his Cossack hunter Thoma Lephikin he climbed down into the yawl among the water barrels; and Bering, caught up in a puckish impulse, summoned the ship's two trumpeters to the rail and had them blow a brassy flourish over the astounded Steller's head.

Kayak Island is long and narrow, lying at a right angle to the mainland; its spine rises to 1200 feet or so, covered with moss above the spruces along shore. The boat steered for an opening where a stream came through the bare gray rocks of the shoreline, and as soon as its keel grated on the pebbled beach, Steller jumped ashore. He was the first man to touch the New World, and trembled with excitement and anticipation.

He left the boat's crew to fill their casks and, with Lephikin, set out in the direction of the mainland. Presently they came upon a hollow log in which cooking had been done with hot stones, the remnants of a recent meal scattered about and a covered pit with bark utensils and food in it; the people (Eskimos of the Ugalakmiut tribe) had fled into the woods. Steller took samples of everything and sent Lephikin back to the boat with them, telling him to warn the crew that natives were about and request several more men to help explore. He set off again, up hill and down, collecting the plants he came upon, until he came to a high place from which he could see the mainland. This sight brought a sudden feeling of depression upon him, for he was afraid that he would never be able to reach it; and then he observed some smoke rising from a nearby hill. His spirits rose again, for he thought he could learn much from the makers of the smoke; he gathered his collection together and trotted back to the boat. It was just leaving; he asked the crew to repeat his request for help and ask Bering to send presents for the natives so he could prove his peaceful intentions. When the boat had left, he sat down wearily to make tea and describe all the plants he had collected, before they could wither. Many of them weren't new, but he had found a new raspberry, Rubus spectabilis, which excited him so much by its promise of a delicious taste—for it wasn't fully ripe as yet—that he had Lephikin dig up a number of them later with the idea of planting them in a box to be sent back to Russia.

The boat returned in an hour with the gifts Steller had requested to be placed in the dugout; it also brought a message to Steller to get himself back on board or be left where he was. It was only several hours to sunset, and Steller still had a lot he wanted to do. He ignored the order to return, sent Lephikin off to shoot some of the native birds for specimens and took off himself in the opposite direction. Near sunset he returned with more plant specimens and found Lephikin waiting for him with the corpse of a brightly colored bird, now known as Steller's jay. He identified it at once, by an amazing feat of memory, from a drawing of Catesby's of the American jay from the Carolinas he had seen in the Academy at St. Petersburg, and although it was not the same bird, the two are somewhat similar. It was a bird unknown in Siberia, and because of this and his recollection of Catesby he was now positive that he was in America.

The boat's crew had the final order for him to return or be left. His prizes were stowed aboard, he and Lephikin climbed in, and the boat got under way. The sun was setting as they reached the ship; Steller, prepared for a great row for staying away so long, had the wind taken out of his sails when he climbed aboard and Bering again offered him chocolate. His belligerence evaporated;

143

he had had the greatest day of his life and no one was going to quarrel with him after all. This time he joined the chocolate drinkers.

Half an hour later Khitrov returned to the ship, to report that he had found a good anchorage as well as a native hut on Wingham Island, which he had circumnavigated and landed upon. The hut had been made of hewn boards and had held various pieces of native property and a stone with copper stains upon it, indicating that it had been used as a whetstone for copper tools. He hadn't encountered any natives, but had brought back with him some of the things he had found—a wooden vessel, a paddle, a fox tail and the whetstone.

chapter
nine

BEFORE GOING TO bed that night, Bering and Steller had a long conversation, for Steller was terribly afraid that he was not going to get enough time ashore and tried to convince the Captain Commander that he should have it. During the day Bering had managed to throw off the awful depression that had long been gathering upon him, but he was tired now and the depression had come back; his feet were swelling again, as they seemed to be doing so often lately, and the lassitude that had been increasing as the voyage had stretched out was brought more sharply to his mind as the strong, eager young man before him talked enthusiastically of what he wanted to do. Lying on his bed, watching Steller walk excitedly up and down in the dim light of the cabin lantern, he thought of home and the warmth and comfort of it as a thing infinitely desirable and impossibly far away. He had always respected learning; tired and ill as he was, he realized more than he ever had before the scientific zeal that burned in Steller. He had often been impatient with the man, but this time he was gentle with him.

He had complied with his instructions, Bering said; he had discovered America, and now had to think of getting safely home to report his discovery. It had taken them seven weeks to get this far, and it might take them longer to return. He feared that the prevailing winds would soon shift to southwesterly—a fear that was later borne out—and give them a great deal of trouble. In any event, the decision of the ship's council on May 4—to return to Kamchatka toward the end of August or by the middle of September at the latest—was binding upon him, and gave them only three weeks to sail along the coast of the New World and examine it for harbors, rivers and so on for whoever was to come after them. They were alone; Chirikov, who was to help them if they got into trouble, was God knew where; Bering had brought Steller to investigate the minerals of the New World, he continued, but when Steller got ashore he spent his time shooting birds and digging up bushes, spending his time looking at things that would still be there when the next ship came to America. The instructions of the Admiralty mentioned a mineralogist; he couldn't understand the importance of what Steller was doing in the light of his instructions, and he wasn't willing to hold the ship in one place while Steller did it.

There was little Steller could say in the face of this logical and calm capitulation; it brought him to silence in spite of the revolt and frustration that filled him. He went up on deck while he still had control of his temper.

This talk before going to sleep cleared Bering's mind of the indecision that had been plaguing him when he sent Khitrov ashore for water, and early next morning he got out of bed, went up on deck and issued orders to get under way westward. It was most unusual for him to do this, especially at such an hour and without consulting his officers. Waxell, who had the watch, suggested that they fill the remaining twenty barrels with water before leaving; but Bering said they had enough and doubtless would be able to get more along the coast if they needed it. He thought the weather was going to change, and wanted to get away from the land before it did. The anchor was weighed, topsails, foresail, jib and topmast staysails were set and they moved off. The rest of the day was fair and they continued in sight of land, but the next morning the weather grew stormy, as Bering had predicted it would, and they stood further out and lost sight of the coast in the fog and rain. It was still foggy on the twenty-fourth, three days later; Bering called a consultation with his officers and it was decided to hold a southwesterly course during the fog to keep off the land, and change it to a west-by-north course when they could see the coast. On the twenty-ninth they had to heave to for a blow; it began to clear on the thirtieth, and on the thirty-first the course was set toward where they thought the mainland should lie. They had been off soundings since the twenty-seventh, and had passed the entire length of Kodiak Island in the fog without seeing it.

Fog came down on them again on August 1; and shortly after midnight on the second, as the fog thinned out enough to allow them to see a little by the dim light of the last quarter moon, they suddenly discovered that they were close to land. All hands were hurriedly piped up to get sail on the ship to bring her about in the darkness and trailing mists, when the leadsman reported that they only had four fathoms of water under the keel. The crew, which had grown oddly lackadaisical during the last week or so, were slow in obeying orders and some of them were very clumsy on the ropes. It was touch and go for a few minutes, but they managed to claw their way out into eighteen fathoms, where they anchored for the night. The situation was not reported to Bering.

The next morning the fog lifted long enough for them to make out an island about a mile away; Waxell and Khitrov named it Foggy Island, but it is known as Chirikov Island today. Steller wanted to go ashore again, but Bering refused him, and there was an argument. Steller said that the Academy would blame him severely for not investigating any land they came to, but Bering took care of that. He called a ship's council, where it was read into the minutes that no one was to accuse Steller of not being eager to do his duty on all occasions. The fog cleared toward noon and it turned warm and calm, and around eight in the evening, when the wind came up from the southwest, they weighed anchor.

They held a course to take them toward the coast during the night, and early the next afternoon, through the fog that had held during the day, they sighted Mt. Chiginagak, the high, snow-covered volcano near the beginning of the Alaska Peninsula. There seemed to be land all around them, and that fact coupled with the constant fog brought the officers to a decision to turn south. On the fourth they sighted the Semidi Islands, where the water was full of seals, sea lions, porpoises and sea otters. Rain came on to join the fog, and for the whole week they didn't dare go near the land and made slow progress; after the seventh the wind shifted to the west and gave indications of staying there. Bering's fears of headwinds were being realized.

Nor was that all. The inefficiency of the crew, which had been increasing, was explained at last by the undeniable symptoms of scurvy. This disease, which laid the constant shadow of apprehension on the minds of sea captains in those days, came from vitamin deficiency, the lack of fresh food, damp and depressing living conditions and hard work. The body cannot cope with the demands made upon it, and a dreadful lassitude, combined with a feeling of gloom and apprehension, visits the sufferer. The onset of the disease is insidious; there is a loss of weight and progressively developing weakness and pallor. Presently the gums begin to swell, then get spongy and bleed, and the breath becomes very foul. As the disease develops and no steps are taken to check it, there are hemorrhages into the muscles, joints, kidney and bladder; the spleen enlarges, ulcers sometimes develop in the colon, the skin gets dry and rough and a severe anemia develops. The patient grows increasingly weaker until he cannot get about, and does not even want to try. He merely lies in his bed, in an uncaring stupor, and befouls himself. Arthritic symptoms and great pains in the joints are usually present.

Manifestations of the disease developed among some of the men so rapidly that by August 10 the ship's apprentice surgeon, Betge, was sure enough of his diagnosis to report that five of the crew had scurvy so badly that they were unfit for duty, and that sixteen more of them were affected; these sixteen would surely go down sooner or later if conditions weren't changed for them. In reality all of them, including Bering himself, were showing indications of the disease, and in the light of Betge's report something had to be done. Bering called a meeting of his officers.

They reviewed the meeting in May, at Petropavlovsk, when it had been agreed to turn home in September, and came to a decision not to wait until then. Autumn was already beginning and the prevailing winds, which had shifted to the west, showed signs of change; they were a long way from home, scurvy had broken out, and the exploration of the American coast, which they had intended to make, was practically impossible because of the constant fogs and storms which hid from them an unknown coast peppered by thousands of islands and shoals. They would start home at once, as close to the fifty-third parallel as the wind would permit, to see how far the American coast extended toward Kamchatka. The petty officers were called in, and agreed with the decision. Steller was not consulted, but argued anyhow that a more southerly course would be better. Time proved him wrong; for although the ship was driven down to the forty-ninth parallel and even below it before the end of the trip, there were still westerly gales to contend with. Bering's fears had been all too well founded.

From the tenth until the twenty-sixth the track of the ship resembled an erratic, wandering course around three sides of a square; it took them down almost to the fifty-first parallel before they turned northward again; the wind had settled generally into a westerly or southwesterly direction, to give them constant trouble. Their average sailing distance for this time was only about seventeen miles every twenty-four hours, and as they estimated that they were over 1200 miles from Petropavlovsk, if things kept on as they were going, it was going to take them two and a half months to get home, being blown all over the ocean as they went.

This was a cheerless conclusion not improved by the fact that their water was by now down to twenty-five barrels. Another meeting of the officers was called and it was decided, as the American coast as they last saw it was around 55° or 56° north latitude, to change course to find it again and take more water aboard. On the evening of the twenty-eighth sea lions and gulls, signs of land, were seen; they hove to for the night, got bottom at seventy-five fathoms at four in the morning, and moved off north again. At eight o'clock a large number of bleak islands came into view with

the mainland thirty or forty miles behind them. They stood in toward them and the yawl was sent to look for a good anchorage;
by eight o'clock *St. Peter* was anchored between the Nagai and
Near islands. At three o'clock in the morning the glow of a fire
was seen on Turner Island, two and one half miles away.

Khitrov, who had the morning watch, sent first mate Eselberg
and a crew in the longboat to Nagai at sunrise with ten empty
barrels for water, and asked Steller if he wanted to go along.
Steller had from the first been very outspoken about his poor
opinion of Khitrov, and expected nothing from him; he suspected
that Khitrov planned to go to Turner Island to see if he could
find the fire builders, and wanted him out of the way. He wanted
to see the fire builders himself, having already formed a theory
that they would be related to the Chukchi and the Kamchadals;
but he also suspected that Khitrov wanted the honor of being the
first man to see the Americans and wouldn't take him along.
Rather than stay on the ship, he agreed to go with Eselberg, taking Lephikin, his Cossack, and Plenisner, his artist, with him.
The boat moved back and forth with the water barrels, and at
one o'clock the sick were sent ashore for a change.

Steller had been right in his suspicions, for as soon as his boat
moved away, Khitrov suggested that he take the yawl and a crew
to investigate the fire builders. Waxell, who was in command
because Bering was too sick to be on deck by now and had great
difficulty using his legs, didn't like the idea; he doubted that
Khitrov could get back to the ship in such a small boat if a sudden
blow came up; but Khitrov was very insistent and finally demanded that his request be put in the log. At this Waxell went
to Bering, who said that Khitrov should be allowed to go if he
was so anxious to do so, and was to take some presents for the

natives with him. Khitrov got off at eleven o'clock with five men, including a Koryak or two who spoke sufficient Chukchi to interpret.

On Nagai, Steller, who knew the great necessity of having good water on the ship now that scurvy had broken out—especially as the ship's medicine chest didn't contain any antiscorbutic then known—first searched for springs, found several of them, and went back to the beach to guide the water detail to them. To his horror, he found the detail filling the casks from a brackish pond close at hand and tried to stop them. They paid no attention to him, having heard too many arguments between him and the officers, but he managed to get them to take samples of water back to the ship with his protests as a physician anxious to preserve his own health as well as the health of others. The answer that came back, chiefly on Waxell's responsibility, was that the pond water was a little brackish but good enough and the casks were to be filled with it.

This was a fatal mistake, and Waxell afterward admitted that it had disastrous effects upon the scurvy-ridden crew. His excuse was that he was worried at the time about the anchorage and wanted to load the water as quickly as possible, and that if the worst came to the worst, they could at least cook with it. He refused to listen to Steller. The bitter truth lay in the clash of personalities between Steller and the naval men. They didn't understand one another, and Steller hadn't helped matters during the trip by quarreling with them about nautical matters with which he had had no experience; they on their own part had come to look upon him as a nuisance, to be ignored.

At any rate, they continued to load the brackish water, which would be very bad for the men, who were already getting too much salt from their diet of salted meat and fish. Steller made another effort to dissuade them, and failed. There was one other thing he could do: he asked for a detail to collect enough anti-scorbutic plants for them all. This request was turned down like the others, and Steller gave up. He and Plenisner and Lephikin went off to explore the island. While they were moving about, one of the sick crew members who had been brought ashore at one o'clock, a sailor named Shumagin, died. His death set the pattern for many more; for a number of the scurvy sufferers, who seemed to hang on to life while they were undisturbed, died when they were brought up from the increasingly foul miasma of the hold into the open air.

Steller and his companions found the place, as well as all the other islands they could see about them, to be rocky and treeless; the low bushes and shrubs crept along the ground and were inter-twined and crooked; there were surprisingly tame foxes and marmots and a large population of birds which had not yet started on their southern migration. It began to rain in the late afternoon, and Steller started to build a hut in which to spend the night, but decided finally to go back to the ship for one more try at convincing the officers of how important it was to collect the antiscorbutic plants. He got such a churlish reception for his pains that he decided to say no more about it, collect enough plants for Plenisner, Bering, Lephikin and himself, and let the rest of the crew do without.

The next morning, which was August 31, he and Plenisner went ashore again with the water detail; as before, the sick were sent along to spend the day. The unfortunate Shumagin was buried and the island was named for him. By noon the wind began to freshen, as Waxell had feared it would, and at six was blowing so hard that the longboat was sent to take everyone off. The surf was so high that it was extremely difficult to load the sick, and Steller and his party had to wade out up to their waists in the icy water. By midnight there was a northeasterly gale and worry and confusion aboard, for Waxell was afraid that the anchors wouldn't hold and Khitrov was still ashore and couldn't be abandoned. By noon the next day, when the blow abated somewhat, there was three inches of water in the hold and more men on the sick list, while those who had been ashore were worse from the soaking they received getting back on board. The following morning the wind shifted to southeasterly and picked up again, and the anchorage had to be shifted to the lee of the Near Islands.

Khitrov, meanwhile, had found the site of the fire but no natives. He tried to get back to the ship on the thirty-first but couldn't make it in the little yawl and had to land on Nagai, breaking up the yawl in the surf. They built a fire to dry themselves and signal the ship; when St. Peter shifted anchorage, they feared they were being abandoned; it was not until September 2 that the longboat could be sent for them. The officers, belatedly thinking that Steller might be right about the water, sent a few barrels along to be filled from a spring for their own use, but with the difficulties of embarking the castaways, these barrels had to be abandoned.

With Khitrov aboard again, after holding them up for three days, they tried to get to sea. Khitrov, full of high spirits at his rescue, elected to heave the lead and lost it on the first cast. This in itself seemed a bad omen to the superstitious sailors, and became a worse one when someone recalled that it had been exactly a year since he had lost all the ships' biscuit at Okhotsk. There was little wind, however, and they had to anchor again. The next day the wind was no better, and after drifting about, *St. Peter* finally dropped anchor at her former anchorage. The five days they had wasted waiting for Khitrov and the wind after he came aboard would have saved many lives later on; for with these days they could probably have made Avacha.

St. Peter had scarcely got the anchor down and everything secure when there were shouts from the rocky island to the south, and soon afterward two small boats appeared moving toward the ship. As they came closer it could be seen that they were kayaks like those used by the Greenland Eskimos; they each held one man. When they got to within hailing distance they stopped and the men began to shout long speeches in a language none of the interpreters could understand. They were the first Americans the explorers had ever seen; they lined the rail, excited by the strangers, shouting back at them and gesturing invitations to come aboard. This the natives declined to do, but made gestures indicating that the sailors should come ashore. One of them paddled closer, and, reaching into his shirt, found some dark, shiny substance with which he painted his face. He then stuffed his nostrils full of grass and, reaching down, came up with a red stick which he floated toward the ship. The sailors tied two Chinese tobacco pipes and some glass beads to a board and floated it toward him; he picked it out of the water, gave it to his companion and, cautiously drawing near the ship, held out an eviscerated falcon tied to another stick. The Koryak interpreter had a piece of Chinese silk and a mirror, which the native wanted placed in the falcon's claws so they wouldn't get wet, but the interpreter instead pulled on the stick to bring the native closer. This frightened him, and he drew away. The mirror and the silk were thrown to him, whereupon he and his companion paddled toward the shore beckoning for the sailors to follow.

There was an immediate conference on board about following the natives to learn more about them. Waxell, who wanted to go, went below and got Bering's permission, and a boat's crew was made up of Waxell, Steller, the Koryak interpreter and nine soldiers and sailors with cutlasses and guns hidden under a piece of canvas. The boat pulled away, but when it reached the beach it had to stand off because of the rocks and the surf. There was a crowd of men and women, all of whom gathered at the water line with welcoming gestures. The sailors didn't want to chance the boat, as it was the last one they had; so the interpreter and two of the men undressed and went ashore through the surf, taking the anchor with them on a line. They were received deferentially; whale blubber was pressed upon them, and one of the natives launched his kayak and came out to the boat. He was given a cup of vodka, which he tried to drink and immediately spat out angrily, and then a lighted pipe, which he liked no better. These two mainstays of civilization were enough for him, and he went scowling back to shore.

The wind had increased while all this was going on and the landing party were ordered to get back to the boat, but the natives had decided to keep them ashore; they first pressed more whale blubber on the visitors and then began to restrain them by force. Several natives took hold of the anchor cable and began to pull the boat ashore. This unpleasant situation was resolved by Waxell's quick order to shoot over the natives' heads; they all fell down in terror, the landing party ran for the boat, and the natives stood up again, picked up stones from the beach and gestured for the sailors to leave. The anchor cable was hurriedly cut and the boat returned to the ship with its somewhat shaken crew, who had come close to spending the rest of their lives ashore. The people with whom they had had their adventure were Aleuts, Aleutian Eskimos. In his journal Steller described them very thoroughly, although he had only fifteen or twenty exciting minutes in which to observe them, and deduced that they were of Asiatic origin.

There was a violent storm during the night, and the next day the wind dropped and hauled around more to the west, so the anchorage was changed again. Late in the afternoon nine kayaks came out in single file; two of them approached the ship, and the natives in them presented sticks decorated with falcon feathers and some of the lead-colored face paint. They were given a rusty iron kettle, five needles and some thread, which they passed around among themselves and returned to shore. When they got there they built a big fire and screeched loudly for a while before darkness hid them from view. It was the last the voyagers saw of them.

On the sixth the ship got under way again, passing the island to the east, and moved out to sea. There were great clouds of birds on the northern side of the island: auks, puffins, snipe, gulls and others unknown to science. The mainland dropped below the horizon in the afternoon, and they began to encounter a large number of whales that were so restless and active that everyone began to fear that dirty weather was on the way.

It arrived the next afternoon, when the wind came up and increased so much that they had to shorten sail; by evening they were in a roaring storm that lasted all night, tossed them severely about and brought them down to the spanker. The antiscorbutic plants that Steller had been feeding Bering for the past few days had helped the Commander so much that he was beginning to regain the use of his legs, but the condition of the rest of the sick list had grown worse from the tossing about the ship suffered during the storm. Conditions below were deteriorating badly; the scurvy patients, constipated by their disease, were having bloody fluxes from their bowels, and no one had the time or energy to attend them. The hold stank horribly, and between conditions aboard and the realization of how late the season was, how few miles they were making westward and how far away they were from home, there was a sudden, severe drop in morale. There was some talk of trying to winter in Japan or America, which came to nothing, and the bad water and lack of antiscorbutics increased the sick list.

For the next two weeks, on a southerly course, they fought the east wind, having squalls, storms and much wet and drizzly weather to bedevil them. By September 22 they estimated that they were down almost to the fiftieth parallel, and a north-westerly course was resumed. The second to die was a grenadier named Tretyakoo, on the twenty-third. On the afternoon of the twenty-fourth, which had been a gloomy day, they raised land over the bow; it looked like a long group of islands backed by a snow-covered volcano thrusting into the cloudy sky in the distance. As they had only reached 51° north latitude, this dismayed them, for they didn't know about the southerly curve of the Aleutians and hadn't expected to see land until around 56°, where they had left it; they were frightened and considerably sobered to think what would have happened if they had come upon this land in the night. They were probably around Adak and Atka.

Course was changed to get away from the land; that night the wind came up and developed into a violent storm. They could do nothing but scud before it, fearful of losing the masts. There was a lull on the twenty-sixth, although the sea remained extremely turbulent, but the storm returned on the twenty-seventh and built up to such fury that no one remembered having ever experienced anything like it. The ship reeled and tossed, out of control, and shuddered as though taking cannon fire; her people were helpless and didn't think they would survive it. The storm continued all the next day with more violence than ever and there was hail and rain with it. They hoped for a lull on the twenty-ninth but didn't get it; during the night the wind shifted to the southeast, and then back to the west, and the storm continued. At five o'clock on the morning of the thirtieth a new storm from the southwest fell upon them with such terrifying violence that they were sure they were going to die. No one among those still on their feet could remain at his post and they all began to be a little crazed; it was impossible to cook, and the soggy, half-burnt biscuits they had all been living on began to run out. The storm roared on; St. Elmo's fire ran along the rigging, and a third of the crew was down; the teeth of the rest of them were loose and Bering lost the ground he had made up under Steller's ministrations. It was not until the thirteenth that the storm began to blow itself out, but they had lost invaluable time as they were blown all over that part of the ocean, and had been driven down below the forty-ninth parallel and back eastward nearly seven degrees of longitude; the ship's track during the storms looks like a cat's cradle.

Inevitably the question of wintering in America came up again, but Bering—who was now down for good with scurvy—refused to consider it. He knew that they couldn't survive it, and thought that they might make Avacha. He ordered collections taken up among the Russians for the church he had caused to be built in Avacha and among the Lutherans for the church in Viborg, and the northwest course was taken up again. They had been fearfully shaken up and the threat of death had been constantly with them since September 26. Scurvy was making terrible progress, and conditions in the hold were unbearable. The grenadier Kiselev died on the nineteenth, the servant Kharitonov on the twentieth, and the marine Zaviakov on the twenty-second. On the twenty-sixth thirty men were down, and two more were added to the sick list next day. The weather was turning cold, and it began to snow. The second mate, Yushin, a tough and enduring man, wrote in his log: "I have such pains in my feet and hands, owing to the scurvy, that I can with difficulty stand my watch."

There now begins to appear discrepancies in the various logs kept aboard, as though those who kept them were too miserable and exhausted to be accurate. Yushin and Steller say that they sighted the high, snow-covered island of Kiska on the morning of the twenty-fifth; Khitrov says they sighted it at four in the afternoon. Three days later Stepan Buldirev, the cooper, died, and as another island (now thought to be Buldir) appeared out of the fog, they named it St. Stephen. In the fogs and storms that were falling upon them they were moving from the Pacific into the Bering Sea, and they all knew how desperate their situation was. Nearly all the drinking water was gone, so Khitrov proposed that they anchor and send the longboat ashore for a new supply. The other officers vetoed the proposal, realizing that there weren't enough able-bodied men to raise the anchor again once it was down or handle the boat.

The mistakes had been made in the past and now the results of them were appearing, like a note falling due: the time wasted searching for that baseless delusion of the geographers, Gamaland; Khitrov's loss of the biscuits, which would have allowed them to winter in America and escape the storms and adverse winter winds; the days lost searching for St. Paul and waiting for Khitrov to get off the island after losing the yawl; Waxell's decision about the water, and the refusal of a detail to gather antiscorbutic plants. Bering had been correct in his estimates of how the Expedition should move, in his fears of the autumn change of winds and the insurmountable difficulties accompanying it; if he had not been worn down and broken by the monstrous task put upon him, the overambitious plans of the Academy and the fact that the Admiralty had refused him the necessary authority, he might well have had them home.

All this was beside the point now. He was dying; the shadows were beginning to gather around him in the fog and unending dampness and cold, in the wailing, snow-laden wind that held them away from home and the fearful storms that wracked them; the mephitic reek from the hold crept into his cabin as he lay full of pain thinking of the wreck of his life, the 6000 miles of Siberia crossed so many times, the pressures from St. Petersburg and the nightmare years at Yakutsk.

chapter

ten

THE FOG OF sickness and exhaustion, like the fog of war that confuses soldiers in battle, deepened on the ship. On the twenty-ninth, at seven-thirty in the morning, they sighted high land, which turned out to be an island or islands. No one seems to agree on how many there were. Steller saw two, and thought the day was the thirtieth; Müller, in his history taken from sources current at the time, arrives at three, and Waxell saw two, agreeing with Steller against the log that the date was the thirtieth. Yushin's log says there was only one. Waxell also thought that the islands he saw resembled several of the Kuriles at the northern end of the chain. Apparently these islands were the Semichi, but their names are relatively unimportant; their fancied resemblance to the Kuriles, upon which Steller agreed with Waxell, further confused them on their reckoning (which was already confused enough because the weather had been so thick that they had been unable to take observations for a long time) so disastrously that they thought they were south of Avacha and turned their course northward again. They were lost; being so bedeviled by illness and blown about, not having any familiar point to check their reckoning upon, they all had different ideas as to their location. If they had sailed to the west instead of to the north they would have reached Avacha in little more than a week.

The confusion continued and grew deeper. The log says that the northern course, which took them to 54° 07′, was changed to westward on November 1; Waxell and Steller agreed against the log that they had reached the fifty-seventh parallel on the third, and the two deputy commanders, Waxell and Khitrov, found it hard to agree upon anything.

All this is understandable in view of the weather and the crew's condition. Men were dying every day. Karp Pashennoi, a soldier of the Yakutsk garrison, died on November 1, the carpenter Petrov on the second, the drummer Chentsov, the grenadier Popov and the soldier Davidov on the fourth. Later that morning the grenadier Nebaranov died in a cold rain that soon after changed to snow. The living had come to such a pass that the man who took the tiller had to be helped to it by two others who could still manage to walk, and little sail could be carried because too few were in condition to handle it. The ship often lay wallowing, dead in the water, and if really bad weather had come up, it would have finished them. It rained and snowed. The men begged to be let alone so that death would finish their troubles, and Waxell exhorted them instead of issuing orders.

Shortly after eight o'clock on the morning of the fifth a range of high, bleak and snowy hills appeared through the fog; and as they thought they were in the vicinity of Kamchatka, a wild, feeble rejoicing broke out on the ship. Dying men crawled up from the stinking hold, and even Bering, who was an extremely sick man, was roused from his semi-comatose condition; pitiful little cups of brandy, saved through all the vicissitudes of the trip, appeared among the crew. Some of them thought they recognized the coast near Avacha; Khitrov loudly congratulated himself upon the perfection of his navigation; but as the land came nearer, there began to be some doubts because the great volcanic cones behind Avacha harbor were not visible. Then, as though in mocking irony, the sun came out, gave them their first observation in ten days and blasted their hopes. Their latitude was 54° 30′ and should have been 53° 10′. They were too far north to be home.

The saw-toothed profile of the land, rising 1500 feet precipitously out of the sea, still seemed to be the mainland; an opening like the mouth of a bay appeared against the background of hills fading off into the fog from the northwest, but it was too late in the day to try to get into it. The wind was freshening from the northwest, and rather than find themselves on a lee shore as darkness came down, they spent the night in tacking to try to hold their position.

By dawn the next morning, as the squally snow flurries whirled about them, they had tacked to the north far enough to see that what they thought was an entrance to a bay was in reality the open sea between two islands, known today as the Commander Islands. There was no mainland. The northern end of Copper Island, from their evening position, had covered the southern end of Bering Island and made the two islands look like a continuous coast in the fog. They were still lost, and very soon discovered that that wasn't the worst of it; all the mainstays to starboard, rotted by the endless dampness, had parted during the night and the main shrouds to larboard with them. No one on board was well enough to replace or splice them, so they had to drop the main topsail and lower the main yard to avoid losing the mainmast. The wild enthusiasm of the previous day gave way to despair.

An inspection of the remaining running and standing rigging showed that none of it would last much longer; there was little food left and only six barrels of bad water. When Waxell and Khitrov reported all this to Bering, he roused himself sufficiently to order a general meeting of officers and men in his cabin to consider what they should do. Waxell and Khitrov were for going ashore, with the hope of somehow surviving the winter there; Bering didn't agree with them. They had suffered terribly, he said, but couldn't they manage to hold out a little longer and try to make the mainland?

The officers said it was impossible. The rigging was breaking all around them; there was hardly a man able to stand on his feet, and the winter weather was daily growing worse. There was nothing to do but go ashore and hope that God would preserve the ship for them until spring. A vote was called for, and although the men said that they were beyond working, they would follow Bering. Steller claims that at this manifestation, Waxell and Khitrov began to threaten the crew beyond Bering's hearing—a sort of bullying of rickety skeletons by other rickety skeletons—until the crew gave up; the final decision was to winter on the island. At this, officers and crew alike set course for the island and crawled off to their fouled bunks to sleep, in excruciating pain and utterly exhausted, not caring what happened to them.

Steller stayed on deck alone, at the tiller, until afternoon, when it looked to him as though they wouldn't get to the island before dark. He went below and asked Bering if he could order an officer to the deck; Bering sent him with the order, a few of the crew were rounded up, and about sunset they managed to get the anchor overboard. They were within view of a sandy beach; the wind and waves had quieted and it seemed as though they would have a good night. Half an hour later, however, the sea came up suddenly with such violence that the ship was tossed around like a cork, and broke the anchor cable. Pandemonium took over; screaming and wailing arose from the ship, and the spare anchor was thrown over. It snapped its cable at once. The waves broke over the wallowing ship until Waxell thought the deck would be stove in; the ship bore down on the reef which the falling tide revealed between them and the shore, smashed down twice upon it, was lifted over by a huge wave and came to rest in the quiet water beyond the rocks. The last anchor on the ship was thrown over, and held. In the sudden quiet and calm there was nothing for the terrified crew to do but wait for morning.

The wind died down and the first quarter moon gave them enough light to see the shore; they were between two curving arms of land; the sandy, gently curving beach was not over 300 fathoms away, backed by hills that rose gently to the mountains dark against the sky in the distance. They were safe for the moment; most of the desperately sick men managed to think that they were at last on the coast of Kamchatka, and after the trials and terrors that had beset them they again fell into an exhausted sleep.

Later on they realized that there was no other point on the entire circumference of the island where the ship could have found a harbor, and if they had been carried in sixty yards further to the north or south, they would have landed on shelving rock and been quickly broken up and killed. The next morning, of course, they didn't see this. Twelve men had died and forty-nine were very sick; there was hardly any water, good or bad, and it was a question of whether there were enough men strong enough

167

to launch a boat to send ashore to get any. They were not in a real harbor but merely between two arms of land, and as the tide came in over the reef, the surf grew rough and the ship began to wallow again. By eleven o'clock, after terrible exertions, they managed to launch the longboat, and Waxell and Steller, with Plenisner and Lephikin, got ashore in it.

What they found was not very encouraging. There was a stream of good water at hand, but no trees grew on the island except the Arctic willow, which was only several inches high and sent out small branches along the ground; they would have to depend upon driftwood, and what driftwood there was was covered with snow. This put them in a position of having little wood to burn and none to build houses out of; but there were sand hills along the stream with deep little valleys pitted with fox dens between them, and the explorers decided there was nothing to do but stretch the rotted canvas over these pits for the men to crawl under. Waxell and the Cossack returned to the ship to report to Bering, and Steller and Plenisner stayed ashore.

The accounts of that day and the next are very confused. Waxell was so ill that he moved about like a man in a daze, and Steller (who, with his artist Plenisner and his Cossack Lephikin, were the only well men on board because they had been eating the antiscorbutic plants) seems to have collapsed several days into one.

At any rate, he explored a little while Plenisner shot a few ptarmigan to stew for the sick. They also managed to gather some plants for Bering and the crew, and built a little hut from what driftwood they could find. The animals they encountered were so fearless and tame that Steller was soon convinced that they were on an uninhabited island. Many sea otters came out of the surf to stare at them, and the blue foxes, which seemed to come from everywhere, gathered in crowds to bark and sniff at them, and finally grew so bold that they had to be driven off with kicks and blows of the ax.

On the eighth the crew, calling up the strength of desperation, warped the ship into a better position and put out several grapnels to hold her. At four o'clock in the morning of the ninth the boatswain, Nils Jansen, died, and at eight Khitrov gathered part of the crew. Some of them died when they got out into the fresh air on deck, but he finally went ashore with ten of them and several dead bodies to bury. They began to enlarge several of the fox dens that Steller had found among the sand hills along the creek; their intention was to shore up the interiors of them with driftwood to keep the sides from falling in and roof them with canvas from the ship, but until they could finish them they had to lie in the snow on the beach in a circle, the living with the dead, with a little fire burning in the center. As soon as they could crawl into them they did so, to get out of the wind and the weather, and work on them as best they could.

Some of the men had died in the boat and several more died when they got ashore; the foxes moved on these corpses and ate the hands and feet off them before they could be buried; others stole everything they could carry away, gnawed the soles off boots and pulled the baggage around. Steller and Plenisner killed sixty of them that day, with little trouble, and stabbed a few more that tried to pull the dead beasts out of their hands as they were skinning them. More and more of them appeared, and they were a great nuisance as long as the crew was on the island. They crept into the dugouts at night and stole things, nibbled the fingers and toes of the sick, undermined poles that meat had been put up on so that they fell down; it was almost impossible to keep things away from them. The men grew to hate them so thoroughly that as they improved a little in health they killed and tortured them at every opportunity—punching out their eyes, breaking some of their legs, half skinning them and letting them go, singeing half their fur off. None of these cruel practices drove them off, and there were a great many blind, two-legged or flayed foxes always running about with the others.

It was decided to bring Bering ashore in the afternoon; and because some of the sick had died as soon as they came up into the fresh air from the foul hold, he was carefully wrapped up, carried by four men in a sling and laid gently in a roofed hollow of his own. Steller and his party were impressed by their captain's air of stoical composure. Apparently he had realized that he was going to die, and faced his end with calmness and serenity.

For the next few days the business of taking the sick ashore and working on the dugouts went on, as the waves would allow it. Waxell had decided to stay on the ship with what men they hadn't got off, and took up his quarters in the galley, where there was a little warmth from the fire he could keep burning. He thought he would be able to manage better there, but it was a mistake; the horrible stench and foul air from the hold penetrated to him, and soon he lost the use of his legs. Several men died during that time and had to be thrown overboard; they were so short of water because the boat couldn't get to them that they had to collect the snow on the deck and melt it. It was not until the twenty-first that they were taken ashore, and when they carried Waxell up from the hold, he covered his face with his watch cap because so many of the crew had died as soon as they got to the air.

Khitrov had managed to stay on his feet, but he went down as soon as he was ashore. He was put to bed with Waxell and the rest of the enfeebled, yellow-faced invalids, and it was thought for a few days that he was going to die. Steller, Plenisner, Lephikin and the few men who were still on their feet were kept busy nursing the sick and killing foxes, birds and sea otters to feed the invalids—most of whom found it almost impossible to eat because their mouths were so sore. The gums of most of them were almost black, spongy, and so swollen that they covered the teeth.

On the night of the twenty-eighth a violent storm came up from east-southeast, broke the anchor cables that held the ship, drove her on the beach and stove in her port side below the water line. Although some of the supplies, the flour and groats, were ruined, a good supply was saved. It was taken as the final calamity at the time, but it was really a great stroke of luck; for the ship couldn't have lived at anchor all winter, they couldn't have unloaded her, and if she had been driven out to sea, there wouldn't have been any timber to try to build another ship in the spring to get them off the island. No one thought of this at the moment, however; the rise and fall of the tides soon buried her to the wales in the sand and filled her with water, and they gave her up. In their despairing frame of mind, without timber or a hope of rescue, they sent out two parties, which managed to stagger to higher ground and confirm Steller's suspicion that they were on an island, out of sight of the mainland, and there was no one else on it.

When this was reported, the morale of the crew, which was very low, sank even lower. They wept because they were cold, unable to eat without great pain, and without hope: the foxes gnawed at the increasing number of corpses and attacked the sick; driftwood was very difficult to find under the snow; and the weather grew colder and promised worse to come. The officers, who had managed to stay on their feet and nurse and encourage them, had finally broken down; whatever discipline they had managed to maintain ended. The crew's mounting hatred for everyone who had got them into their terrrible condition focused upon Khitrov —who was, indeed, responsible for a good deal of it. He had been put out of Waxell's cave because there wasn't room enough, no one wanted him and no one would build a dugout for him. He was finally forced to settle in with the crew, which cursed and reviled him. For a few days it looked as though Waxell was going to die, and everyone who could nursed, treated and fed him, desperately trying to pull him through so that the command wouldn't fall to the hated Khitrov.

The dugouts were finally finished and covered with canvas. There were five of them: a big one, double-roofed, for the crew, one for Waxell and several other men, one for Steller and his party and two more. They were damp, crowded and cold, but better than nothing, and two barrels from the ship were placed at the entrance of each of them to put meat into away from the ever-present foxes. Driftwood poles were stuck into the sand around them, and clothes were hung on there to dry on the few days that the sun came out.

Bering, despite the fresh food and attention that could be given him, grew weaker every day. He was sixty years old and his once splendid constitution had been too knocked about by hardship, worry and killing work to cope with the disaster and the scurvy. He had developed a rectal fistula, which opened and became infected, and this was followed by gas gangrene and dropsy. His mind remained clear; he bore his pain with stoical dignity, constantly thought of the crew and hoped their luck would be better than his own. He sent out another scouting party on December 1 to make doubly sure that they were on an uninhabited island. On December 7 the sand from the walls of his dugout began to slide down and partially cover him; when Steller and the others came to remove it, he requested them to leave it, for he felt warmer with the sand over him. He died early on the morning of the eighth, and was buried the next day.

So ended, on a bleak and empty island, the life of the Dane whom Peter the Great had chosen to explore the North Pacific and find America. In the sixteen years he had given to the search he had made mistakes, as every man makes them, but he had accomplished much under immense difficulties. He had always been considerate of those under him; he had the respect and liking of everyone he had ever commanded. Steller says that he was too lenient with his officers and crews, and then in the next breath admits that a harsher man would have allowed a heartless exploitation of the natives and ruined all Siberia. Bering had said that a younger, more active and resolute man should have conducted the Second Expedition, but the concensus of opinion of those who knew the circumstances is unanimous that the Expedition would have fallen apart under anyone else.

chapter
eleven

Now THAT BERING was dead and buried near his adjutant, a commissary and two grenadiers, the command fell upon Waxell. He was still too ill to exercise it, and most of the others were in no better shape. They were completely miserable; scurvy had them down, prostrate and shivering in their dank holes in the sand with the foxes to plague them. Steller, Lephikin and Plenisner had to nurse them, hunt for meat and gather driftwood from under the snow along the beach. It was extremely difficult to find, and more than once they went without fire and ate their meat raw. They ate the foxes when they had to, but sea otters furnished most of the meat.

These beasts, which are true otters, are about five feet long, and were extremely plentiful on the island; they came up on the rocks and beaches at low tide singly or in groups to sleep or play. Their fur is very beautiful and durable, being first among furs in the scale of hardness, as the diamond is among gems. The Chinese loved sea-otter fur and paid very high prices for it.

They were so tame and unsuspecting at first that the castaways could creep up on them as they slept and beat them to death with clubs. Their meat was tough and sinewy, rather like leather, which could be swallowed eventually after they'd chewed it long enough—which, of course, was very difficult because of the soreness of the scurvy-ridden men's gums. With this tough meat as their main diet they looked with longing eyes on the sea cows, huge aquatic beasts like the manatee, which came in near shore in herds when the tide was high to graze on seaweed. But the sea cows weighed anywhere up to four tons, and while they would have furnished good meat for a very long time, they were far too big and strong for sick men to get a harpoon into, much less to handle after they did it.

They were very fortunate that the sea otters were about in such great numbers and so easy to kill, and that there were a great number of ptarmigan, which were also tame enough for a time to be killed with sticks. Otherwise they would have been left with little except the rye flour and groats from the wreck, and this wouldn't have helped the scurvy as the fresh meat would; even though it was soaked with sea water and had hardened in its leather sacks, they pounded it to powder again, stirred it up with water, let it ferment for a couple of days and then fried it in oil in little cakes. They apportioned the meat sparingly, having decided to save about 800 pounds of it for the attempt to make the mainland the following summer.

November went by in utter wretchedness, and most of December. Several more men died, bringing the total to thirty out of the original crew of seventy-eight—a remarkably low mortality in view of the terrible conditions they had to face. Toward the end of the month the survivors—having had rest, all the meat they could eat and good water—slowly began to recover. Snow continued to fall, and when it wasn't snowing it was so damp, with an average humidity of eighty-six per cent, that the temperature, which hovered in the low twenties with an occasional low near zero, always felt much colder. It is amazing that they could stand it, under the conditions in which they had to live. There were frequent and violent hurricanes, and several times men who had to crawl out of their crowded, dank caves to answer a call of nature were almost carried away.

There arose, of course, the problem of discipline as the men began to feel better. Their position seemed pretty hopeless to them; they had suffered a great deal, and were understandably bitter about the people who had got them into their predicament. They were not in the least inclined to acknowledge authority any longer and, left to themselves, might have taken out their feelings on Khitrov and one another if Waxell hadn't handled them with great skill and patience. He induced them to view their existence as a co-operative one, and by his own enterprise and cheerfulness he steadied them and gave them an example to follow. He was helped a good deal in this by Steller, who worked well with him, and who had set up his own household in shifts, assigning two men to cook, two to clean up, two to gather wood and so on—an arrangement that worked out so well that the other households began to follow the same scheme.

By Christmas Day things had settled down into a routine, and most of the crew had recovered sufficiently to think of a celebration. It was not very elaborate; they made a cake of sorts of their soaked flour, drank tea in the absence of anything better, made speeches and even sang a few songs. Having somehow managed to avoid freezing to death, drowning or starving, wretchedly housed, they huddled together for warmth and thought for a while of home and what they would do if they ever got there, away from the freezing winds, the snow and the wild, leaden ocean

177

that held them prisoners on their bleak and comfortless island.

The next day the three men sent out by Bering before his death returned. No one had ever expected to see them again; that they had managed to survive at all was a testimonial to their extraordinary toughness and hardihood. Their report was not encouraging. They hadn't been able to walk all around the island; cliffs came down to the sea in many places, and aside from the flotsam cast up by the sea they hadn't found a single evidence of humanity on the beaches they walked along. From almost a month of wandering, however, they were sure that it was an island on which they were all marooned.

Their report further depressed everybody, coming as it did on top of the reaction from the Christmas celebration. One of the men who was still sick, Panov, died on January 2, and on the seventh the scurvy claimed its last victim in the ensign Lagunov. After these men were buried, the crew could see nothing in front of them for many months but short, dark days, storms and cold; they had to go farther and farther from camp to find wood, and when they found it, to carry it home on their backs, and when the day's work was over there was little to occupy them. As their physical condition improved and they found a little energy not taken up by the hard work and miserable monotony of their lives, they began to look about for something to do, and presently they found it: a rage for gambling took hold of most of them. They had played cards while they were ill to pass the endless time when they couldn't do anything else; now they began to play in earnest. At first they played for money, which meant little to them, and then they began to play for sea-otter skins, which would be very valuable if they ever got ashore. They played as long as they had enough light; the men off duty were always playing, and when they weren't playing they were slaughtering sea otters to skin. As the sea otters were thinned out and frightened away from the vicinity, some of the unlucky gamblers began to steal from the lucky ones, and quarrels broke out.

Steller, who was at heart a conservationist and hated to see the sea otters butchered and their meat thrown away, complained to Waxell about the situation, reminding Waxell that gambling was forbidden in the Russian Navy; he wanted the gambling stopped. Waxell listened to him, and refused to do anything. The men, he said, had had a very bad time, and this was a reaction from it; he didn't intend to interfere with them. What could he do, in any event? Discipline was gone, the officers were considerably outnumbered, and it was no time to stir up a mutiny. Khitrov, who was getting about again, sided with Waxell; he was profiting from the gambling. In his journal Steller wrote some bitter things about the naval officers, by which he meant Khitrov; he always got along well with Waxell, whom he admired and with whom he worked very well.

During January the men recovered more rapidly, and by the end of the month most of them were on their feet again. The gambling fever abated somewhat, but because the sea otters were harder to find now, they were sometimes rather short of food; they even ate the intestines of the otters they could catch, and often were reduced to the rank and fishy meat of cormorants. Early in February they had a great windfall: it was discovered that a dead whale had been washed ashore several miles away, and they all turned out to hack hunks of blubber from it and lug them back to camp. It was not as fresh as it could be, but they cut the hunks into little squares and boiled these in sea water until most of the oil ran out of it, and ate the nerves and sinews that remained, without cooking; the oil helped them get it down. This sort of thing was eked out by what little flour they allowed themselves and by the few antiscorbutic plants that Steller could find under the snow at this time of year. Waxell notes that the slim diet was a little difficult for him, for he had his twelve-year-old son with him and he and the boy counted as one man on the ration allowances. It is about the only time that he mentions his son.

By February firewood had become a serious problem, and they were going ten or twelve miles along the beach for it. The canvas they had stretched over their holes in the sand had become so rotted by the perpetual dampness of the sea fogs and snow that it gave way before the violence of the gales, tore and blew away, leaving them under the open sky. When it snowed, which it did frequently, they learned to lie still under a rug or a blanket and be covered by it; it was warmer under the snow. There were also several earthquakes during the winter which shook the sand down on them and nearly filled their holes; all of them who were ambulatory had to turn to quickly and dig out the sick, and excavate their own burrows again.

By March the sea otters were so frightened of them that they couldn't be approached any more, but by that time the fur seals had begun to appear on the western shore of the island to bear their young and mate. They came in great numbers, and although their meat was strong, extremely tough and bad-smelling, it sustained them. Occasionally they were able to kill a young sea lion, which had good meat; it didn't constipate them and make their bellies swell as did the meat of the other marine animals. When the fur seals left, the hair seals began to come in, and a little later in the spring another dead whale, over forty feet long and fresher than the first one, was washed up and solved their supply problem for quite a long time. They dug in the snow for crakeberry bushes, boiled them in water and drank the infusion for tea.

It was about this time that the mating season came on for the foxes, which occupied these thieving beasts enough for a time to give the crew a little rest from their constant depredations. Food took second place in the foxes' interest; everywhere a man looked they were coupling or tearing one another up in ferocious fights. They howled and snarled and yowled like cats, and for a time added their uproar to the wailing of the wind.

When the snow began to leave the ground in March and the early green shoots of herbs and plants appeared, they collected and ate them or boiled them. Steller guided them in this enterprise, and this time they listened to him; they had all seen how the plants he had tried to make them collect on the Alaska coast had kept him healthy. In his journal Waxell admits his original mistake: they didn't really feel healthy, he says, until they had the green plants to eat.

During this time of short, stormy days, hurricanes, snow and cold their chief concern next to keeping life in themselves was the ship and how they were going to use it in escaping from their island prison when the weather settled. As early as the middle of January they held a ship's council of all the men who could totter to it to talk about the matter; for although the old shipboard discipline was gone, none of them could forget that the ship belonged to the government, for which they held a fearful respect that had been with them all their lives. Shipboard discipline was one thing, but the government was another; and when they dealt with government property they had to proceed with care and formality. There was an interminable conference, at which it was suggested that they put rollers under the ship and float it, but a difficulty arose: there was no timber big enough to make rollers. The next suggestion that they dig a trench from the ship out into deep water fell through when it was pointed out that they had no way to keep the sand from falling into the trench as fast as they dug it. This kind of thing went on for a while, and then Waxell suggested that they break *St. Peter* up and make a smaller boat out of her timbers.

This notion terrified the more timid crew members and met with considerable resistance, but it was finally decided that there was nothing else to do. Four days later another council was called at which everybody signed the agreement except a demoted lieutenant named Ovtsuin, who had been on one of the Arctic-coast branches of the Expedition; he read his dissent into the record. On the twenty-seventh he submitted a longer, detailed dissent; on the twenty-ninth it was finally agreed by everyone except Ovtsuin to break up the ship in March.

There was still hope, despite all this, that the ship was usable as she was. On February 1 a very high tide with a violent gale behind it carried the hull higher up the beach, and as the water stayed in it, there was hope that the bottom was sound; but they soon found out that it was not, that the water stayed in because the hull was full of sand.

A week later there was another earthquake, and as they were well enough now to discuss it, somebody put forward the idea that they might be in Kamchatka after all; there were earthquakes in Kamchatka, and whatever explorations they had already made had just not gone far enough. There was nothing further they could do about the ship until the weather improved, so they decided to explore some more and be sure that they were on an island before breaking her up. Yushin, the second mate, was appointed to head a party of four men, and on the twenty-fifth they started north along the coast. Yushin was instructed to proceed to 56° 10′ latitude, where the Kamchatka River entered the sea. The party returned on March eighth, saying that it was impossible to get past a sheer headland forty-seven miles from camp, and reported that they had seen an island or land to the east about forty miles away. This report was pure fiction and not taken very seriously, for it was thought in the settlement that the five men had done more sea-otter hunting than exploring. Another party was got together, headed this time by boatswain Ivanov, in whom everyone had more confidence.

He was told to cross to the southern side of the island and follow the shore until he came to the island's end or reached the mainland. He was back in four days, having been stopped by impassable rocks, so his orders were changed and he was sent out again. This time he was to follow Yushin's route as far as he could along the coast, then cross whatever mountains he came to and proceed to the south coast and move along that coast until he came to the end of the island or reached the mainland. Steller and three men of his household decided to go with him, and they moved along together until they came to the Lyesnaya River, a few miles north of the settlement, where they parted company. Steller's company crossed the island to Gladkovskaya Bay, on the southern side of the island, through a sort of pass made by the valleys of two short rivers running in opposite directions from the height of land in the middle of the island; it was a rugged trip, but not as bad as over the mountains. They found that the sea otters in the bay, which hadn't been hunted, were comparatively easy to kill; it opened up a new source of food for the settlement. It was only a twelve-mile trip, but until well into the spring it was quite dangerous, for any party making the trip was liable to be caught on the way by quick and violent storms that dropped snow up to six feet deep on them. On one occasion four men making the trip were caught in such a violent storm that they could hardly keep on their feet and couldn't see a yard in front of them. They had to sleep all night under the snow, and by morning they were so stiffened by the cold that they could hardly dig themselves out. One of them fell into a brook and spent the night in it; his clothes were frozen stiff on him by morning, and for a time it was feared that he was going to lose his hands and feet. Another went blind for a time through exposure. Steller himself almost lost his life twice on these trips. To make it and get back, burdened with sea-otter carcasses, through the rocky country and the murderous squalls from the sea, was a triumph of courage and luck.

Ivanov's party got back to camp on April 6, and reported that they had definitely settled the matter of being on an island. There was no further question in anyone's mind, and now they could proceed with breaking up the ship.

On April 9 there was a council to settle the arrangements for breaking up St. Peter. The twelve men most expert at handling an ax were to keep constantly at work on the hull; the others were to keep the camp supplied with meat and firewood and attend to the household, while Waxell, Steller and Khitrov were to oversee matters in general and lend a hand when necessary.

Another dead whale washed up; it was so big that its blubber supplemented their supplies the rest of their stay and they even had a little of it left when they sailed from the island. This last whale raised their spirits considerably, and the start of the work raised them even more. They set hopefully to work; grindstones were dressed, tools cleaned and sharpened, a smithy was put up and they began to make charcoal to use in it.

After the work got well started under Waxell's capable direction, Steller began to spend more time investigating the flora and fauna of the island. As spring came on, all sorts of birds and beasts which hadn't been there in the winter began to appear. Guillemots returned to their rookeries on the cliffs; red-throated loons, white-breasted auks and colorful-crested sea parrots whistled and cried and flew about. Hutchinson's geese and many species of ducks swam in the sea, and Lapland longspurs, snow buntings and sky-larks sang and flew about on the tundra. Steller observed and collected them; the larger birds made welcome additions to the menu and the smaller ones brought the feeling of spring and hope with their songs.

He collected several skins and described the Spectacled Cormorant, a rather stupid, flightless bird only known on Bering Island, which was to be killed off and extinct by 1850; he was the only naturalist ever to see it alive, and now its skin is rarer in museum collections than skins of the Great Auk. He also spent a great deal of time in the fur-seal and sea-lion rookeries, in a little hut for concealment among the uncountable thousands of the animals, and wrote in great detail reports on their lives, matings and habits which have since been regarded as the standard work on the subject.

These studies absorbed him; he was having a wonderful time; but as the weather moderated and the snow began to melt, he and everyone else was interrupted in their work as the creeks suddenly became roaring torrents and flooded everything. All of the snow packed in the narrow valleys made a tremendous run-off, which was added to by a series of heavy rain storms. The settlement was flooded along with everything else; water rose two or three feet in the dugouts, and they had to be hastily abandoned and shacks built on higher ground. The only benefit that accrued from this tribulation was the melting of the snow on the beaches, which exposed a great deal of firewood they hadn't been able to find before; it relieved them from hauling wood for great distances on their backs.

The fact that wood was much handier to them underlined the continuing difficulties in getting sufficient meat, and brought their attention again to the sea cows that fed up and down their beach. They had been unable to cope with these huge beasts before; weakened by scurvy and able to catch enough sea otters, they had eyed the great creatures hungrily and let them alone, but now they decided to make a serious effort to catch some of them. They repaired the ship's remaining boat and, having plenty of rope and a working forge, made great iron hooks and put them to the test.

Four or five men went out in the boat with a strong sailor in the bow holding the hook, from which a line ran ashore. The sea-cow herd, feeding on the laminaria below the surface, came up to blow occasionally but paid little attention to the boat. When a cow surfaced near the boat, the sailor in the bow drove the hook into it, and everyone in the boat began to stab it with bayonets and beat upon it with whatever was at hand. Practically the entire command ashore was on the rope, and they pulled the struggling beast toward the beach. It thrashed violently about, great fountains of blood spurting from it, and the rest of the herd rallied around trying to upset the boat or break the rope; the desperate enterprise went on until the sea cow was pulled ashore and dispatched by the entire command's stabbing and beating upon it.

Here at last was superlative meat, and plenty of it. The cow weighed at least 6000 pounds; the fat was sweet smelling and better than butter, and the meat was savory and as good as the best beef. It was remarkable in that it would keep without spoiling even in hot weather for many weeks; their need for good meat was solved at last.

As June brought the tide of plants and swiftly blooming sub-arctic flowers to cover the island's rocks and tundra, Steller spent a good deal of his time botanizing, collecting and cataloguing the flora, and making short excursions here and there. Mostly the weather was cloudy; there was only one completely sunny day in the month, but as July came in, the weather improved. There was another earthquake, and after the camp was put in orderly shape again, Steller decided to make an extensive exploration of the island. He found the northern seal rookery and the seven-mile-long lake at the island's northern end, the northern plateaus so different from the jumble of 2000-foot peaks in the south. All in all, he got a gretty good idea of the island, and reported to Waxell when he got back that although he had prospected for metals and minerals on his travels he had found none.

After his return he dissected and described the sea cow—the only scientific description of the animal we have, for it was quickly exterminated by the fur hunters who came to the island after *St. Peter*'s crew got back to Kamchatka. It was a tremendously difficult operation, for the animal weighed around four tons and none of the sailors whom Steller had nursed back to health during the winter would give him much help. The foxes were a constant trouble to him; as soon as he would cut out an organ and turn away from it for a moment, they would make off with it, along with his notebooks and everything else they could carry. The weather was rainy and cold, and he had to work in it. He himself couldn't draw, and had to call on Plenisner to do his drawings for him. In spite of great difficulty he didn't take notes but wrote his complete anatomical description, and it is a brilliant piece of work. This paper finally reached St. Petersburg, but the drawings that were made on the island never reached the Academy. They were lost somewhere in transit, in the dreary wastes of Siberia.

chapter
twelve

ALTHOUGH ALL THREE of the ship's carpenters had died of scurvy, there was a Siberian Cossack named Staradubtsov in the company who had worked under Spanberg while Spanberg's ships were being built at Okhotsk, and he volunteered to try to build the new boat. The stern and sternpost were up early in May, but the work went slowly; the weather was bad, there were problems about food and firewood, and every step of the construction had to be agreed upon by everybody. By the end of May the keel was laid and the frame timbers were set up, and early in June the work of planking began. Salmon began to run up the rivers and many were caught in nets to augment the supplies; with plenty of food, better weather and bright prospects of getting off the island before the end of summer, morale began to soar and men worked hard and well. The hull was ready by July, and they caulked it with tar obtained by trying out lengths of tarry rope from the wreck. Supplies were got together: meat salted, bread baked, water casks repaired.

The new ship, a one-masted hooker thirty-six feet long, with a twelve-foot beam and a depth of a little over five feet, was finished by the end of July, and as they looked at her they knew that they were going to be very badly crowded when they all got aboard. It was also evident that all the government property salvaged from *St. Peter* wasn't going to go on her, and it frightened all of them to think of leaving government property behind. There were long conferences as to whether it would be better to carry the stuff and leave some of the men, or carry half of it and leave men to guard what was left until the ship could return. No one wanted to be responsible for deciding who was to be left, or how this was to be decided; Waxell finally settled the whole thing by calling a ship's council at which it was decided to build a storehouse and leave everything they couldn't carry with them in it, without guards. They all signed the decision of the council, and noted in the minutes that they had come to the decision because the island was uninhabited.

The next thing they had to decide was how much baggage every man could take with him. There was a great stock of furs, including about 700 sea-otter skins, which would be very valuable when they got to the mainland, and as they didn't know how far they would have to sail or how long it would take them, there had to be plenty of water and supplies. The total burden was fixed at three and a half tons, and midshipman Sind was appointed to work out everyone's baggage allowance from the lists they all handed in. Rank, as usual, had its privileges; Waxell was allowed the most, Khitrov came in next, and Steller came in a poor third with half Waxell's allowance and seventy pounds or so less than Khitrov. This was very hard on him, for he had gone to inordinate trouble to prepare the skins and skeletons of a young sea cow, a sea lion, a fur seal and a sea otter; he had many other specimens and a huge collection of plants; he was finally told that there would be no room for any of these things. He begged, pleaded, argued and shouted, as any scientist would have done, and got nowhere. Finally he admitted that there really wasn't enough room and asked if he could take small pieces of skins and skeletons, but even these were disallowed. All that he was able to take with him were plant seeds and a pair of masticatory plates from the mouth of a sea cow, which are now in the Academy of Sciences in Leningrad, the only ones in the world. The skin and skeleton of this beast would be priceless and unique now.

The launching stocks and the ways, which caused a great amount of trouble because of the shortage of wood, and which had to be extended for 175 feet because of tides and other conditions, were ready on August 8, and as a high tide would be in shortly after noon, the crew gathered for the ceremony. Prayers were offered up for success, and the boat was christened *St. Peter* after her predecessor. When they tried to launch her, the platform upon which she was to slide down the ways broke down under her weight, and the ship stuck. Calamity stared them in the face; they had a boat but possibly could never get her down the ways into the sea. They worked like madmen all through the tide to no avail and gave up in despair when the falling tide left them. At high tide the next afternoon, however, they managed to get her launched, and the bleak island echoed to their rejoicings. They found that she drew about three feet, and anchored her in three fathoms. The morning had been windy, with rainstorms, but the weather cleared in the afternoon, and after *St. Peter* was finally riding at anchor, Waxell gave a party at which the main delicacy was saturan, a drink made by pouring boiling water over a paste of roasted flour and sea-cow fat.

They worked around the clock on the tenth and the eleventh

to set and rig the mast and yards, put up the rigging, blocks and sails, install the rudder and take their supplies aboard. This work was finished on the afternoon of the twelfth, and the baggage was brought aboard. They all went ashore again to set up a wooden cross that had been made over Bering's grave, and returned to the ship for good.

Once aboard, they discovered how really crowded they were going to be. Waxell, his son, Khitrov and Steller filled the little cabin to bursting, and the men in the hold had hardly any sleeping space between the cargo and the deck. They had to crawl over one another; as there were three watches, two sleeping spaces were assigned to every three men, and even then they had to throw overboard pillows, clothing, blankets and whatnot to make enough room. While they were doing this they could see the foxes moving into the dugouts and shacks ashore, ransacking them and feasting on the meat that had been left.

At six o'clock the next morning, August 13, 1742, they decided to get under way. The wind was from the north, so they had to warp out of their little bay. This entailed raising the anchor and carrying it out in the boat for every 100 fathoms that they made, but by eleven o'clock they were clear; the anchor was stowed and sail put on *St. Peter*. They sailed between Bering and Copper islands, well pleased with the way their little ship handled, seeing for the last time the shore they had so often and so wearily hunted for wood and meat, the difficult heights they had climbed to search for other people or the dim loom of the mainland through the fogs and the snow. By evening they were off the extreme point of the island; by noon the next day all they could see of it was the jagged high rocks of the southernmost point. They estimated that the mouth of the Kamchatka River was their closest point on the mainland, but decided that instead of heading for it they would make for Avacha Bay.

The headland fell below the horizon and they sailed into the night before a mild southwesterly wind. On the fifteenth a strong head wind came up, and the heavy boat they were towing gave them so much trouble that they decided to cut it loose before it could damage the ship. At about noon they noticed that the hooker was leaking, and they found that they had to have one pump going all the time. By afternoon the water was rising so fast in the hold that both pumps wouldn't hold it. Their only boat was gone, and after all their suffering and trouble, the long winter and the building of the ship, it looked as though they were going to drown almost in sight of the mainland. They quickly formed two bucket brigades and bailed from both hatchways, and sent the carpenter into the crowded hold to find the leak. They began to throw things overboard to lighten the ship, and performed prodigies of effort in clearing working space below. They finally found a hole from which the caulking hemp had been washed by the sea, caulked it from the inside and nailed a cleat over it. Their last brush with incipient disaster was over.

They raised the beautiful snowy cone of Kronotskaya volcano, on the Kamchatka River, on the morning of the seventeenth; it hung in the sky above them as they closed the coast and turned south. They hoped for a quick trip to Avacha, but the winds turned contrary and finally they took to the long oars they had brought from the island; they rowed for twenty-four hours, and reached the mouth of Avacha Bay at two in the morning on the twenty-sixth. At eight in the morning a few Kamchadals came out in their skin boats, bringing news of the world with them—the first news the mariners had had for fifteen months. At two in the

193

afternoon they dropped anchor in the inner harbor. They were home; they went ashore, thanking God to be in a land they had never thought to see again.

The first thing they learned was that their belongings, all the things they had left behind in Petropavlovsk, had been sold and scattered; after Chirikov had returned, having lost men and boats to the savages, been attacked by scurvy and blown all over the sea, everyone had given them up for dead and never expected to see them again. They had lost their possessions, but they had encountered so much trouble and privation and were so fortunate to be home at all that they bore this final loss almost with equanimity. The next morning they held a solemn thanksgiving service, and later on the crew covered the icon in the church with a case of pure silver, inscribing it in gratitude for being delivered from the barren island and returned to the Kamchatkan shore.

Finding plenty of provisions at Petropavlovsk, Waxell decided to leave half the crew there to follow by the first ship in the spring and sail on to Okhotsk in order to get his report of the voyage to St. Petersburg. He had *St. Peter* recaulked and sailed from Avacha Bay on September 2; but less than a day later they encountered such violent winds that they decided the hooker was too lightly built to trust further at that time of year and returned to Avacha. Waxell began to work on his maps and report at once, and as soon as there was snow enough for sled travel he sent them overland by Ivanov to Bolsheretsk, from where they were sent on to the Admiralty. They didn't reach St. Petersburg until August 1743.

In March, Waxell and the crew went to work on the hooker, doubled her bottom with one-inch birch planks and recaulked her, and took off in May for Bolsheretsk, where he stayed out of the way of drift ice in the Sea of Okhotsk until the middle of June, and reached Okhotsk on the twenty-seventh of that month. He, his son and the rest of the crew went on to Yakutsk and wintered. The next year they went on to Yeniseisk and joined Chirikov, who was now senior officer of the Expedition and had established his headquarters there, awaiting orders to return to St. Petersburg. When he got them, in 1745, he went back to the capital and left Waxell in charge—and there Waxell and his crew sat until 1748, when he was recalled. He took the surviving members of the crew with him, and they reached the capital in January 1749. The Second Expedition was over; it had taken the bureaucrats on the banks of the Neva six years to get around to ordering him home. This was not due altogether to laziness and incompetence, however. After Peter the Great's daughter, Elizabeth, had ascended the throne in 1741, supported by the old aristocracy who had never held with the westernization of Russia, there was a great upheaval in the government. Governmental offices and departments fell into chaos, and many things that had interested the old administration interested the new one not at all. Many restrictive measures were put into effect, and thousands of people were exiled to Siberia. The Germans in the Academy, who had insisted upon continuing in their old contentious, superior fashion, fell out of favor; everyone was fed up with them and they were replaced with Russians who were mostly chauvinists or political appointees. The Expedition, or what was left of it, was only one of the things that was neglected in the general change.

After Waxell got to St. Petersburg, however, they did better by him. He was promoted to fleet captain second class that year, and later made captain first class. He was put in charge of collating the journals of the Expedition's ships and the making of a map of the North Pacific, then given command of a number of ships in the Baltic, and finally put in charge of the great naval station at Kronstadt in 1758. He died in 1761, and his widow was given a pension; she and Lavrentij, the son who had been with him and who was by now a fleet captain in the navy, were given a gratuity of 2000 rubles. Lavrentij and Waxell's other two sons were elevated to the hereditary nobility in 1778, and their descendants probably still live in Russia.

The story of the rest of Steller's life is not such a happy one. After *St. Peter* reached Petropavlovsk, he decided not to wait for Waxell and the crew; his task with the Second Expedition was over; so, taking his Cossack Lephikin with him, he set out overland for Bolsheretsk. He arrived there on September 5, and learned that most of his friends in the Academy had been replaced and that conditions were changing for the Academy itself. He had many reports and papers to write and got at them spasmodically during the winter; in the spring he took over and taught in a school for Cossack and native children. He was still sympathetic toward the Kamchadals, and got embroiled in an affair having to do with some of them who were treated badly, due to a misunderstood and overzealously enforced order of Spanberg's, which landed him in trouble later on.

That same year he made a trip to the Kurile Islands and wrote a paper on the invertebrates there, which was lost, and several other papers on fishes that he discovered. When he returned he grew interested in the matter of mammoth tusks and bones which were continuously turning up from northern Siberia and decided to take a trip to the Kolyma and the Anadyr to investigate the mystery of these great creatures and possibly to find one still in a frozen condition. He planned to give a year to this enterprise, which shows that he didn't realize the distance he would have to cover or the difficulties of the trip.

He left on July 27 with a servant, went up the Bolshaya River to its source in the moutains and dropped down to the valley of the Kamchatka River. It was late in the year and travel was slow; the travelers had to live off the country, the salmon in the rivers and the berries and roots they could find. Natives fed them unappetizing messes when they encountered them. He botanized on the way and finally reached Nizhnikamtchatsk, the northernmost of the two Russian palisaded forts in the valley. It was over 700 miles to the Anadyr fort from there, across a range of magnificent volcanoes and the low sphagnum-moss tundra in the narrow neck of the peninsula. This dreary country was inhabited by some intractable savages called the Olyutortsi who killed most strangers, but Steller managed to get along with them, and even lived with them for the latter part of the winter.

They must have convinced him that the trip he had planned was too much for him, for he turned south again in the early spring. When he came opposite Karaginski Island off the coast, he decided to cross the ice and investigate it; no scientist ever had before. But the ice broke up when he was partway across; he lost his dogs and his sled and only saved his life by leaping from ice cake to ice cake until he managed to get to shore. He refitted at Nizhnikamtchatsk and headed back toward Bolsheretsk, botanizing and collecting fishes as he went.

It was spring of 1744 when he got back to Bolsheretsk, to find a midshipman by the name of Kmetevski in charge of the few members of the Expedition still left in town. Kmetevski was a quarrelsome fellow who liked to throw his weight around, and he and Steller soon fell into violent disagreement. Steller wrote to the Senate in St. Petersburg that Kmetevski was ill-treating the natives, which he undoubtedly was; Kmetevski wrote the Senate that Steller had, without authority, freed some natives conspiring at rebellion against the Russians. The Senate was interested in protecting the Kamchatkan natives, but more interested in keeping them under control; the abortive uprising when Bering's ships were built was still remembered, so Kmetevski's letter stirred the Senate up more than Steller's did. Orders were immediately dispatched from St. Petersburg to the Irkutsk chancellory to make a thorough investigation.

While this was going on, the annual supply ship from Okhotsk came into Bolsheretsk, and Steller decided to return on her. He was quite ready to go; he suspected that the affairs of the Expedition were being wound up. He had explored all of Kamchatka; Okhotsk and Bolsheretsk—since the lively times when the Expedition was making up—had declined again into dreary little towns run by understrappers with whom he frequently quarreled, and he had been away for seven years and endured innumerable hardships. With sixteen packing cases of specimens and manuscripts he got on the supply ship and went back with her, reaching Okhotsk on August 19. He botanized around Okhotsk for a while and set out for Yakutsk, which he reached toward the end of October.

It was too late for him to go farther with his unwieldy baggage, so he decided to stay for the winter. Yakutsk was livelier than Bolsheretsk or Okhotsk, but certainly not stimulating to the intellect. The winter days were very short, the temperature dropped to fifty degrees below zero, and the inhabitants who had to spend practically all of their time indoors either slept most of the time or drank huge quantities of vodka. He got through the winter, and when the European mail came in in March, he found his official recall from the Academy in it; it had been on the way for a year. There was also some private mail for him: his father had died; the Academy was having troubles; and there were newspaper clippings that worried him. They had apparently been inspired by some enemy in the Academy, and gave him lurid write-ups as a hero who had saved everyone on the Expedition and built the hooker St. Peter single-handed. They were dangerous because they showed him as not holding to the vow of silence he had taken at the beginning of the Expedition; for the Senate had become very fearful that some other nation would intrude itself into the North Pacific and take advantage of Bering's discoveries.

The ice on the Lena broke up in May, and after the river had had time to settle down, Steller started for Irkutsk. Travel in the clumsy river boats was slow, and he didn't reach Irkutsk until early autumn. There were several accusations against him, including Kmetevski's, being held there; but the governor, who was a friend of the Academy and a good amateur botanist himself, was quite capable of assaying the difference between Steller and Kmetevski and dismissed the charges. After he was cleared, Steller decided he had better get back to European Russia, where his detractors seemed to be very active, and left Irkutsk on Christmas Eve. Unfortunately, the governor's exoneration of him to the Senate didn't reach St. Petersburg until August 1746.

Traveling as fast as he could, he reached Tomsk and then Tobolsk, having troubles with the customs at every turn. There was already a scandal about the furs smuggled back from Kamchatka by a number of people who had been connected in one way or another with the Expedition, and the customs service was giving everyone a difficult time; it seems to have given Steller more trouble than most, and he wasn't the man to submit quietly to it. He made himself unpopular with everyone, including the governor in Tobolsk—who held up the exoneration from Irkutsk to get even with him, and intimated to the Senate that Steller was a suspicious character.

Steller finally reached Verkhoturye, the last customs house at the Russian border, had further troubles there, got through, and reached Solikamsk and stayed for a short time with Gregori Demidov, a very rich man who was much interested in botany. Demidov had gardens and greenhouses, and Steller got permission from him to plant a number of specimens in his gardens to grow for a while before they were taken on to St. Petersburg. He had carried some of them thousands of miles and was afraid they would die if he carried them any farther at the moment through the hot summer weather.

Demidov took a liking to Steller and asked him to go along on a botanizing trip into the province of Perm and the southern Urals, a country where the flora had never been investigated. Steller was greatly tempted, but decided to go on to Moscow; he set out, but after he had traveled for a few days he changed his mind, turned around and went back to Solikamsk.

The two men planned to do a book on the flora of the province of Perm, and for several months had a delightful time traveling, making discoveries, gathering plants and bringing home their specimens to plant. Steller, having found a friend who understood him and shared an interest, was happier than he had been for a long time; he did a great deal of work, and had completed descriptions of 680 species of plants in a summary of his botanical observations when a courier from the Senate in St. Petersburg appeared, told him he was under arrest and ordered him to get ready at once to return to Irkutsk and face trial.

Steller was dumfounded, and then outraged that an adjunct of the Academy of Science, one of the most august organizations in all Russia, should be treated in such a fashion. He protested that he had been exonerated by the governor at Irkutsk, he raged about, but it did him no good. The courier, a man named Lupannin, was ready to believe him but was powerless before the Senate's order and gave him a day to get ready for the trip. He had sent on most of his baggage and had little but a single coat, sixty rubles, the specimens he had collected in Perm, the plants in Demidov's garden and a number of rough drafts and notes. The work of years, the specimens he had collected with such toil and hardship, his very notes might all be lost; he couldn't bear to think of someone else getting into his collections and creating havoc among them, and on top of that he was going to be dragged like a common criminal hundreds of miles back through Siberia. He nearly went out of his mind.

In his great trouble, with so little time to settle his affairs, he wrote a long, rather pathetic letter and a report to the Academy, then a *pro memoria* which, in the light of what happened to him, was a sort of testament. He gave all these papers to Professor Fischer, an Academy member who had stopped in to see Demidov at the time, for delivery to the Academy, and started out with Lupannin on the long trip back to Irkutsk.

It was all too easy to become a drunkard in Siberia; it was, in fact, practically standard procedure; most of the inhabitants had their own stills, and vodka was not at all difficult to come by. Steller had been a comparatively moderate drinker in a land of serious topers, but now, under the strain of the things that had happened to him and the feeling that his life and work were being knocked carelessly apart by malicious bureaucrats, he began to drink more heavily. Summer travel was slow; the river boats by which most of it was accomplished had to be pulled against the current most of the time; and on the way Steller had plenty of time for black depression which could in a measure be lightened by the bottle.

The two men, retracing the many comfortless miles that Steller had already traveled several times, finally got to Tobolsk and then Tara. Summer was over by then and the weather daily grew colder; the rivers began to freeze, and at Tara they had to stop and prepare for winter travel to Irkutsk. It was there that another courier from the Senate found them.

This courier was carrying another ukase, which set Steller free and explained why he had been ordered back to Irkutsk. The exoneration from the governor at Irkutsk had been delayed, as we have seen, first by the governor at Irkutsk and then out of pique by the governor at Tobolsk; it had reached St. Petersburg a month after Steller had been reported passing through the customs post at Verkhoturye. In the light of the accusations against him and the orders to investigate them at Irkutsk, the Senate had thought that he was trying to escape back into Russia. The new ukase, besides freeing him, contained orders for him to return to St. Petersburg by any route that he wished to follow, and provided him with post horses.

He started out at once and, as the winter traveling was good, got back to Tobolsk in half the time it had taken him to make the trip out. He was royally entertained by the Archbishop Narozhnitski, who had been a friend of the Archbishop Theophan, who had befriended Steller long ago and interceded for him when he had first come to the capital from Germany.

Tobolsk was a lively town in the winter, full of merchants and government officials who were always ready for parties, where there was good food and plenty to drink. It was famous all over Siberia for such goings-on, and as Steller was in a mood to celebrate, he probably overdid it; he partied with enthusiasm for three weeks. Presently he caught a fever, which rapidly grew worse, and then decided to get off to St. Petersburg. His friends tried to convince him that he should stay quietly at Tobolsk until he felt better, but he wouldn't listen to them. Sick as he was, he crawled into a sled and started off; the Tatar drivers of his sled loafed on the way and spent too much time in roadside taverns while Steller lay ill in the freezing weather outside; by the morning he reached Tyumen, 170 miles away, he was dying. There were two naval surgeons in Tyumen who doubtless did their best for him, but their best wasn't good enough; he died before the day was out, November 12, 1746. As he was a Lutheran, the Orthodox clergymen of Tyumen wouldn't let him be buried in the Russian cemetery; the only Protestant clergyman in all Siberia, a chaplain named Konigshaven, happened to be in town, and he wrapped Steller's body in his own red cloak and buried him on a high bluff not far from the town.

The ground was frozen and so they could only dig a shallow grave. That night some wretched young men of the town dug the body up to steal the cloak and left what was mortal of Steller lying in the snow for the dogs to devour. This was discovered by Steller's friends, who reburied him and moved a heavy stone over his corpse.

Such was the melancholy and untimely end of one of the most

promising scientific explorers that the world had seen. He had the true scientist's inquiring spirit, he had never spared himself, and had made an astonishing number of discoveries from which other men would profit in the years to come, because he had not had sufficient opportunity to prepare them properly himself for publication.

It is difficult to estimate what would have happened to the Second Expedition without him; but he, his Cossack Lephikin and Plenisner were the only men capable of hunting, wood gathering and the tending of the sick when the crew had to come ashore on Bering Island. They would probably all have died without the ministrations of the three men who had kept themselves healthy with the antiscorbutic plants that everyone else had refused to gather. Alaska had been discovered by Chirikov as well as by Bering, but Chirikov had not been able to stop anywhere on the way home, and the discovery of the sea-otter islands would have been unreported by him. By the time Steller and *St. Peter's* crew returned, the Senate had grown weary of the North Pacific and the Academy had fallen upon evil days and had little power or vitality.

It was the sea otter, with its magnificent fur so loved by the Chinese, and the fur-seal rookeries of Bering Island that sent the *promyshleniki*—those wild fur hunters in skin boats held together with twigs and reindeer sinew—back into those cold and foggy seas along *St. Peter's* track to spearhead the eastern march that developed and colonized Alaska. It would certainly have taken place sooner or later, but possibly under another nation and much differently; perhaps history would have been changed and Alaska would now belong to somebody else.

It would seem fair to say that Bering held the Expedition together until it reached the island where he died and that Steller was instrumental in bringing it home from there. Neither of these men had much luck; honors and good fortune eluded them; it was Waxell, who took Bering's place so capably after he was nursed back to health, who was the lucky one.

Epilogue

WHEN BERING DIED he only knew what had happened to two other sections of the Expedition: the crew that had been sent down the Lena in the covered boat *Irkutsk* to explore the Arctic coast to the east of the Lena, and the crew that had been sent to explore the Ob River and the western Arctic coast in the shallop *Tobol*. Neither of these parties had been successful. Of the forty-six men who had started out in *Irkutsk*, thirty-six had died of scurvy on the Arctic coast in the winter of 1735; one of the survivors had rejoined Bering's crew at Yakutsk and was still alive; he was a member of the party in Steller's dugout. *Tobol* explored the mouth of the Ob River for a little way on each side of the river's mouth but couldn't double the Taimyr Peninsula to the west of it because of ice and consequently failed in its mission. One of that crew also rejoined Bering, and was on the island with him when he died.

Bering didn't know what had finally happened to Spanberg, who had successfully made his second voyage to Japan, and he was, of course, equally ignorant as to the fate of Chirikov and *St. Paul*. He never knew that Chirikov had found Alaska early on the morning of July 15, 1741, a day before the clouds had lifted to reveal to *St. Peter*'s crew the magnificent snow-covered bulk of Mt. St. Elias, and had also been followed by death and misfortune.

Chirikov's landfall had been off Cape Addington, but, finding no suitable place to land, they had sailed along the coast until the seventeenth. On that day the beach looked better and Master Avraam Dementiev and ten armed men were sent ashore in the longboat to look about. They were seen to approach the shore, and that was the last anyone on board saw of them. They sent no signals; the ship kept the neighborhood until the twenty-third, when the small-boat with four men was sent ashore to investigate. It never returned; the new continent had swallowed it as completely as it had swallowed the longboat. Chirikov, very apprehensive now, ran in as far as he dared and fired signal guns the rest of the day and through the night. A fire was seen on the beach, and that was all. At noon the next day two men came out in native boats, screamed at the ship from a distance and went back to shore.

Chirikov could do no more, for both of his boats were gone. He was in a very bad situation; he couldn't get ashore again for his men or even to find fresh water, which he needed badly. On the twenty-seventh he called a council of his officers; the decision was forced upon them to abandon the castaways, if indeed they still lived, and return at once to Avacha.

They had a very bad trip, blown about by contrary winds and so low in water that they had to wring it from the sails and try crude methods of distilling it from sea water. They ate boiled rye mush, salt beef boiled in sea water and had a liberal vodka allowance. Scurvy attacked them; some of the crew died, as well as three officers, who were harder hit than the men. When they finally got to the harbor of Petropavlovsk on October 9, Yelagin was the only officer left on his feet; he fired five guns, and the establishment ashore had to send out boats to bring them in. Chirikov had to be carried ashore in a stretcher, and De la Croyere, who had been suffering from scurvy since September, holding himself together with enormous quantities of vodka, died as he was dressing to go ashore.

In the spring of 1742 Chirikov took the ship out again to search for his commander, missed Bering Island, finally gave up the hopeless search off Attu and returned to Petropavlovsk in July. In August he took *St. Paul* back to Okhotsk and turned her over to the port authorities. His trip to America was over, but he had managed to survive.

What happened to Chirikov's two boats and their crews has never been solved; it remains the first mystery of Alaskan exploration.

There are two possibilities to account for the loss of the fifteen men. The first one puts the place where they went ashore at the entrance to Lisianski Strait, at latitude 57° 50', which is the location given by Chirikov in his log; it is very probably correct, for Chirikov's noon sightings and the general accuracy of his observations were good. There is a tidal bore of considerable power and turbulence into the entrance of the strait, and it may be that both boats were caught in it and swamped.

The other possibility has to do with the natives. A number of authorities on the ethnology of the Pacific coast were consulted long after the occurrence and none of them knew of any native tradition having to do with it. In 1922, however, a man named C. L. Andrews published a book about the history of Sitka, as a historic outpost of the northwest coast and the chief factory of the Russian American Fur Company. Andrews assumes the locality of the disaster to be Sitka Sound, instead of Lisianski Strait, and says that there was an obscure tradition among the Sitka

Indians that whites were lured ashore by one of their number dressed in a bearskin. This bearskin wearer played along the beach; the white men landed to kill the supposed bear, which led them into the woods where they were all killed by the rest of the Indians who were hiding there.

For those readers of this book who would like more detail about the two Expeditions, the logs of the ships, the minutiae of building them and so on, I would suggest:

Bering's Voyages, Vols. I and II
F. A. Golder
The American Geographical Society
Research Series No. 2
New York, 1925

and

Georg Wilhelm Steller
Leonhard Stejneger
Harvard University Press, 1936

There are several other books of interest:

Peter the Great
Ian Gray
Lippincott, 1960

Tent Life in Siberia
George Kennan
Putnam, 1910

The American Expedition
Sven Waxell
An English translation, done in London within the last few years, of a Danish book by Bering's second in command on the Second Expedition

Vitus Bering
Peter Lauridson
Chicago, 1889

Narrative of an Expedition to the Polar Sea in the years 1820, 1821,
    1822 and 1823
    Ferdinand von Wrangell
    London, 1840

The Chukchee, 2 vols.
    Waldemar Bogoraz
    Memoir, American Museum of Natural History

The Koryak
    Waldemar Jochelson
    American Museum of Natural History, Vol. 10

Narrative of a Voyage to the Pacific and Beering's Strait
    London, 1831

A Summer on the Yenisei
    M. D. Haviland
    London, 1915

Travels In Kamchatka and Siberia, 2 vols.
    Peter Dobell
    London, 1830

I would like to express my appreciation at this time to Dr. Henry N.
Micheal, who pointed out to me the more obscure books among the
foregoing and thus gave me great help and pleasure.

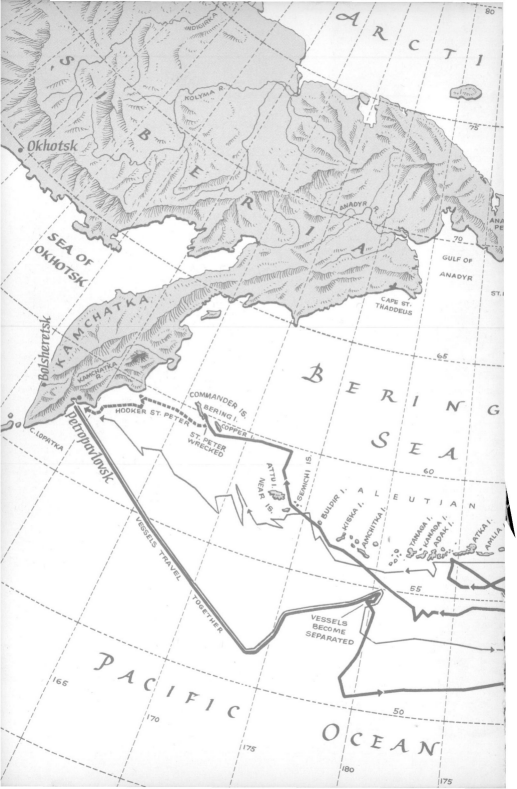